Main Streets of Louisiana

Main Streets of Louisiana

Text by Anne Butler
Photos by Henry Cancienne

University of Louisiana at Lafayette Press
2012

University of Louisiana at Lafayette Press
P.O. Box 40831
Lafayette, LA 70504-0831
http://ulpress.org

Printed in Canada on acid-free.

ISBN 13 (hardcover): 978-1-935754-12-1

Library of Congress Cataloging-in-Publication Data

Butler, Anne, 1944-
  Main streets of Louisiana / text by Anne Butler ; photos by Henry Cancienne.
    p. cm.
  ISBN 978-1-935754-12-1 (hardcover : acid-free paper)
 1. Louisiana--History, Local. 2. Louisiana--History, Local--Pictorial works. 3.
Streets--Louisiana. 4. Streets--Louisiana--Pictorial works. 5. Central business
districts--Louisiana. 6. Central business districts--Louisiana--Pictorial works. 7.
Historic districts--Louisiana. 8. Historic districts--Louisiana--Pictorial works.
9. Community life--Louisiana. 10. City and town life--Louisiana. I. Cancienne,
Henry, 1946- II. Title.
  F370.B87 2012
  976.3--dc23
                          2011049473

Introduction

A Louisiana Main Street Community

They're so different one from the other, these Main Street© communities scattered across the map of Louisiana. The earliest ones developed along the major waterways—the Mississippi and the big bayous—that were the initial highways for transporting crops, goods, and pioneers. Others had to await the coming of the railroad, the tracks reaching inland to connect landlocked prairies to the outside world.

In the southerly coastal communities you can smell the salty sea breeze blowing off the Gulf, with ancient live oaks hung with Spanish moss and the seafood so fresh it's practically dripping. The westernmost ones have more of a Texas influence, while the North Louisiana communities are little islands of commerce and culture set amidst the red-dirt hills, piney woods, and fertile fields of cotton, corn, and soybeans—miles and miles *and miles* of cotton, corn, and soybeans.

The ones that are parish seats of government surround iconic courthouses and town

squares, and the ethnic heritages are French, Spanish, Creole, Acadian, English, Italian, German, and all the other cultural influences that make up this gumbo state of Louisiana. Three are so small they are not even considered cities but are cited as towns in the 2010 census. Populations range from the tiniest, Columbia, with only 390 hardy souls, to the largest, Houma (33,727), closely followed by New Iberia and Slidell. Many of the Main Street districts are also National Register Historic Districts and Cultural Districts.

And yet, as different as they seem, from the cypress swamps to the pine forests and wide-open prairies, they all have one thing in common, a burning desire to hold on to their unique sense of place and to preserve the early commercial corridors that were once the heart and soul of the communities—and sometimes still are. What unites them, in this age of sterile suburban strip malls and characterless cookie-cutter big-box shopping centers, is the struggle to hang on to what makes them different, unique, and so very special.

Most of the Main Street managers who oversee these communities wear many hats—city planner, downtown development director, program director, tourism commissioner, economic development director—in their municipal administrations and they bring to their position incredible expertise in the field, plus the people skills to activate volunteers and encourage disparate parties to work together toward a common goal. Some of these managers are veterans, real pros who have been with the Main Street program since it started; others are more recent

hires, but they all have a passion to preserve significant historic commercial corridors by providing incentives for appropriate restoration and renovation while breathing new life and present-day economic viability into these Main Street communities.

Most of the Main Street managers work closely with their local governing bodies and with both private and public preservation and planning groups on many levels; they are assisted by local boards of directors and supported by community volunteers. Most of the managers are fortunate enough to have enthusiastically supportive municipal administrations, and it certainly helps when there is a local understanding of how preservation and progress must go forward hand in hand, without trampling on each other.

The Louisiana Main Street coordinating program offers support and incentive grants to encourage private investment by providing matching funds to spruce up unsightly or unsafe structures, improve appearances, and encourage new business development that brings new jobs. Local managers are required to attend the annual National Main Street Conference and the Destination Downtown gathering, plus quarterly state training sessions for valuable educational and networking opportunities.

In 1980, realizing that significant historic commercial districts across the country were at risk of being lost, the National Trust for Historic Preservation© established the National Main Street Center, with six states participating initially. Within the program's first twenty-five years, more than forty-three states and 2,200 communities

Church Street, Houma

became involved. The purpose of the program was to revitalize deteriorating and neglected downtowns by focusing on economic development to create sustainable historic commercial districts and introduce new life and opportunities by utilizing existing assets like buildings and infrastructure.

Realizing that these historic commercial corridors were often the hearts and souls of surrounding communities, the national Main Street program determined to provide the incentives and support for revitalizing these districts and to encourage pride in these unique spaces that gave each community its individual sense of place. The slogan "Economic Development That Works" was backed up with statistics showing that, on a national basis, every dollar invested in historic downtowns was multiplied many times over in new private investment, with vibrant downtowns attracting more residents, visitors, and businesses.

Louisiana joined the national network in 1984 with four communities, Franklin, Hammond, Houma, and Donaldsonville. They were quickly joined in the next few years by Minden and Winnsboro. Louisiana Main Street is part of the state Division of Historic Preservation, Office of Cultural Development, in the Department of Culture, Recreation, and Tourism, under the office of the Lieutenant Governor. Director Ray Scriber and Design Coordinator Leon Steele provide support and direction for all of the participants scattered across the state. Today there are twenty-nine Louisiana Main Street communities and four Main Street urban districts in New Orleans, thirty-three programs that are as different as they are alike

in their attempts to improve their areas' economic bases, strengthen public participation, recruit new businesses, and rehabilitate historic buildings for productive use.

The Main Street designation is an honor, but communities must work for it and exhibit the long-term commitment toward sustained economic development through preservation. Property owners within program boundaries benefit from federal and state rehabilitation tax credits, often applied in conjunction with restoration tax abatements that can delay increased property value assessments when historic structures are improved (and hence worth more).

Annual competitive Redevelopment Incentive Grants assist qualified applicants with both interior and exterior restoration and rehabilitation projects. These grants are intended to serve as catalysts for rehabbing and often repurposing historic downtown commercial structures, and they require a matching amount provided by the property owner or applicant; each project is reviewed by the Louisiana Division of Historic Preservation to ensure conformance with strict standards. State grants also support the coordinated Louisiana Main to Main Cultural Roadshow held in each Main Street community throughout the month of November with the idea of encouraging road trips from one community to another by focusing on local history, architecture, music, food, and culture. The Louisiana Main Street program also provides design, organizational, promotional, and economic development services to the designated districts.

In the twenty-five years since Louisiana joined the na-

Main Street, Ponchatoula

tional program in 1984, nearly two thousand new businesses have been started, creating some eight thousand new jobs, with private investments of $315 million and a total investment of over $400 million in historic rehabilitation and new construction. These impressive statistics do not include figures from the four communities that joined the state Main Street network in 2009. Hammond alone, which has been in the state program since it was implemented, has seen more than $56 million in total investments in its historic downtown, closely followed by Natchitoches with nearly $50 million. Two Louisiana communities have achieved national recognition as Great American Main Street communities, Natchitoches and New Iberia; in any given year, only five communities are chosen nationwide for this prestigious honor.

The Main Street approach uses four guiding points to attain a comprehensive revitalization program promoting the historic and economic redevelopment of traditional, mostly rural commercial areas. *Organization* involves building relationships and partnerships among downtown stakeholders, getting everyone working toward the same goal, and assembling the appropriate human and financial resources to implement the revitalization program. *Economic Restructuring* involves helping existing businesses to stay in business, perhaps even expand, while recruiting new ones and providing the necessary support and infrastructure to diversify the economic base. *Promotion* involves marketing the downtown area's unique characteristics and history in a way that encourages consumers and investors to live, work, shop, play, invest, and take pride in

the Main Street district, supplemented by public events and activities designed to draw residents and visitors into the area. Finally, *Design* involves improving the area's image by enhancing its physical appearance, through historic preservation and rehabilitation of the architectural character of downtown structures and creating a user-friendly streetscape.

The National Trust Main Street Center's experience in helping communities bring their historic commercial corridors back to life has shown over and over again that this Four-Point Approach© really does work. This comprehensive approach provides a foundation for communities to revitalize their historic commercial districts by leveraging local assets, including cultural and architectural heritage, local enterprises, and community pride. Why is this important? Because, according to the National Trust, "our Main Streets tell us who we are and who we were, and how the past has shaped us. We do not go to bland suburbs or enclosed shopping malls to learn about our past, explore our culture, or discover our identity."

Our Main Streets are our core, our heart and soul, and as every smart-growth planning and redevelopment study tells us, the larger community is only as healthy as its core. Our Main Streets give us our sense of place and our sense of community. Our Main Streets are what make each community unique and different; they are the repositories of our collective memories. Louisiana's wonderful Main Street communities are all that, and more, because, after all, this *is* Louisiana, with its spicy history blending diverse ingredients into a unique and harmonious whole. We have much in common with all the small historic commercial corridors fighting for life across the country, but, as the Louisiana Main Street slogan says, here it's "just like Mayberry, only the diner sells gumbo and Aunt Bea does a wicked two-step." *Vive la différence!*

Example of rehabilitation in DeRidder

Abbeville

Population 12,257

They call it the most Cajun of places, but Abbeville, with its picturesque downtown squares, has an authentic Old World feel and well it should, having been founded in 1843 by a Roman Catholic priest, Père Antoine Désiré Megret, who modeled it after his hometown in France. On the banks of the Vermilion River, Abbeville was first called *La Chapelle* after Father Megret purchased 160 arpents of land from Joseph LeBlanc and converted the LeBlanc home into a makeshift chapel for saying mass until a real church could be constructed.

The town was incorporated in 1850. Father Megret donated land for the church, courthouse, town square, and surrounding streets, and it was named either for his hometown (Abbeville) or perhaps called *Abbe* (priest) plus *ville* (French for town). He fought to have Abbeville designated as the seat of justice for Vermilion Parish, which transpired in 1854, shortly after the beloved priest perished in a yellow fever epidemic.

Valcourt Veazey, who arrived with Father Megret from France in 1843, began publication of Abbeville's first newspaper in 1852. The paper, called *The Independent*, was sold in 1856 to Judge Eugene I. Guegnon, who changed the name to *Le Meridional*. In its columns Judge Guegnon expressed himself so freely that he was challenged to several pistol duels, in two of which he was wounded. As one of the state's earliest newspapers, *Le Meridional* was published in both French and English until the late 1800s.

Until the twentieth century, Abbeville, like most small rural towns, had dirt streets and wooden structures, many surrounded by fencing to keep out roving livestock. Not

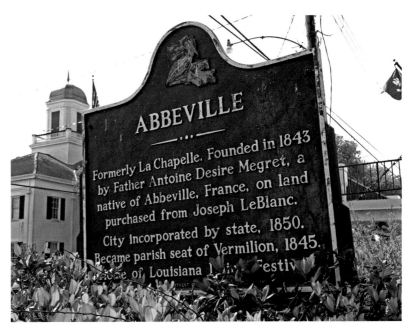

until a couple of devastating fires destroyed much of the downtown area were buildings constructed of brick with dividing firewalls. Travel was most often by steamboat or horse-drawn vehicle until 1892, when the Iberia and Vermilion Railroad (later Southern Pacific) came to town, enabling Abbeville to function as a major rice processing center.

By 1903 some town streets had been surfaced with oyster shells, and some of those were graveled around 1918. Heavy farm wagons and tractor traffic kept the roads so deeply rutted that the local newspaper likened a drive through town to riding a bucking bronco, and the mayor had to scold residents for obstructing traffic by carelessly hitching horses in the right-of-way.

This was, after all, a rural community, dependent on

St. Mary Magdalen Catholic Church

Magdalen Catholic Church, its towering spire dominating the entire townscape, and the two adjacent squares, one for the administration of government and justice, the other for community gatherings and cultural celebrations. Flanked by an unusual 1921 rectory and a cemetery over a century old with some tombstones inscribed in French, St. Mary Magdalen Church is a large brick Romanesque Revival structure that was designed by well-known architect George Honold, who lived in Abbeville for twenty-five years. Listed on the National Register of Historic Places, the church was erected in 1911 as the sixth on that site, some previous structures having been lost to fire or hurricanes. The present church building itself underwent an extensive restoration following a fire in 1981, and today it is an impressive structure with a cruciform interior featuring fine American stained glass windows.

An Italian carved statue of Father Megret stands watch over the church from Magdalen Square. The square, which over the years has been used as a

agriculture and aquaculture, its fields planted with rice and sugarcane or used as pastureland for cattle and the waterways providing bountiful harvests of seafood. This is still the case today, with crawfish farming thrown into the picture to rotate with the rice crop. Abbeville boasts many popular restaurants and oyster bars serving seafood so fresh it's practically still dripping water—Dupuy's Oyster Bar, Shuck's the Louisiana Seafood House, and the RiverFront are just a few of the dozens of fine eateries. Brochures delineate Culinary Trails through Vermilion Parish, and the area is so famous for its Cajun cooking that other attractions feel compelled to advertise "We're more than just a great meal."

Life in Abbeville has always revolved around St. Mary

cow pasture and a setting for street fairs, concerts, and travelling medicine shows, continues to be the central focus of festivities downtown, and its charming fountain and gazebo provide a romantic backdrop for weddings and other social affairs. The Abbeville Cultural and Historical Alliance Center Museum and Art Gallery is a joint effort of several community service organizations, housing art exhibitions, Acadian genealogical materials, and historic documents. Near the museum is The Depot at Magdalen Place in the 1894 railroad freight depot, with railroad exhibits and a gift shop.

The late A. Hays Town, dean of Louisiana architects, designed the brick wall surrounding Magdalen Square. Town also designed the magnificent columned Greek Revival Vermilion Parish courthouse, center of Abbeville's second square and downtown's most distinctive building. The parish police jury and other officials have offices here, while Abbeville City Hall is across the street in a former hotel. Guided historic downtown walking tours in French and English point out all the highlights.

Since becoming a Main Street community in 1994, Abbeville has generated millions of dollars in renovations and improvements to historic downtown commercial structures. Within the twenty blocks of the Main Street district and the several adjoining blocks of residential historic district are a number of architecturally significant structures listed on the National Register of Historic Places. With the help of matching funding through rehab incentive grants, enormous improvements have been made to the downtown streetscape, preserving the historic essence while adding appealing color and charm.

The Historic Residential District that developed between old-town Abbeville and the railroad corridor features structures dating from the late nineteenth and early twentieth century, evidence of the rise in the area's prosperity stemming from the influx of Midwestern settlers and the corresponding boom in the rice industry. The tree-shaded galleried homes exhibit architectural influences of Queen Anne Revival, Colonial Revival, and even Arts and Crafts styles.

Unlike other small towns that grew up along the railroad stations, Abbeville was well established before the iron horse hit town with its central business district already the focus of commerce and major supplier of goods and services for the entire surrounding area. The historic downtown tells the story of Abbeville's development—the central core expanded, with residential neighborhoods developing between downtown and the railroad. Flanking these districts are two eye-catching tributes to the twin economic mainstays of Abbeville: an enormous and rare brick rice mill stands as testament to the large-scale rice production Midwestern settlers introduced into the area, and three gigantic yellow cans of C. S. Steen's Pure Cane Syrup, actually giant holding tanks for the internationally famous syrup made open-kettle style from local sugarcane by multiple generations of the Steen family for more than a century.

The anchor of the historic commercial district is the Bank of Abbeville, a two-story brick Romanesque Revival structure with an arched corner entrance and rock-

Above: Bank of Abbeville
Opposite page: Vermilion Parish Courthouse

faced cast cement stonework finish. Besides its elaborate brickwork, the most unusual features of the building are two soaring towers, crowned with finial-topped metal caps. Restoration contractors say you never know what you'll find when working with old buildings. This was certainly the case in 2011, when construction workers, turning the bank's vacant second floor into office space, pulled some material from a long-unused chimney and out tumbled the bones of a local resident who around 1984 had attempted, for whatever reason, to enter the bank surreptitiously without realizing that the chimney narrowed as it descended.

From this fascinating bank building radiate commercial structures dating mostly from the turn of the twentieth century, comprising what National Register documents call "by far the finest grouping of historic commercial buildings in Vermilion Parish." Most are well detailed in terms of brickwork, and many show Italianate influences, with arched windows, parapets and entablatures, cornices and decorative brick panels, and even some cast-iron columns. The restored downtown structures today house specialty and gift shops, service and governmental offices, restaurants and museums—a thriving business community encouraged through Abbeville's Main Street program.

Next to the bank is Frank's Theatre, a two-story brick structure with parapet built in 1925 that sits empty and awaiting restoration. Here in 1949 was held the southern premiere of *Louisiana Story*, a locally filmed award-winning documentary commissioned by Standard Oil to explore the impact of oil exploration on the life of a bayou trapper. Today theatrical productions are still presented

Frank's Theatre

Abbey Players Theatre

downtown by Abbeville's community theater group called the Abbey Players in the old Vermilion Bar building that once housed an early saloon and brothel.

Not far from the Abbey Players Theatre is a rustic small wood frame structure where in 1918 Italian immigrant Sam Guarino, with a $200 loan from the Bank of Abbeville guaranteed solely by a handshake, opened a blacksmith shop. Donated to the city by his descendants, the structure today offers living history demonstrations in tribute to the gifted blacksmith who for half a century was so happy in his work that he often whistled or sang old favorites like *O Solo Mio*.

Abbeville has plenty of annual festivals designed to keep the downtown area hopping in a joyful celebration of Cajun *joie de vivre* with bountiful helpings of music,

dancing, creative arts, cooking contests, and plenty of good food. There's the Vermilion Carousel of Arts in the spring, the periodic Sounds on the Square, the Daylily Festival and Garden Show in early summer, the Louisiana Cattle Festival in October, and *Les Lumieres du Village d'Abbeville* and the Downtown Abbeville Christmas Stroll in December.

Across Louisiana, most little Cajun communities have their own unique festivals, many celebrating food from okra to jambalaya, gumbo to frog legs, crawfish to cracklins. But Abbeville, situated as it is between the shrimp capital of the world, the duck capital of the world, and the rice capital of the world, knew it had to come up with something spectacular to stay competitive. Following Father Megret's example, the town of Abbeville went back to its Old World roots to come up with an appropriate tribute to its French heritage. In 1984, three members of

Above: Sam Guarino's Blacksmith Shop
Opposite page: Abbeville Giant Omelette Celebration

the local Chamber of Commerce traveled to Bessieres, France, where they were knighted as the first of Abbeville's *chevaliers*. They returned home determined for Abbeville to join an international *Confrerie* of cities saluting their French heritage by celebrating, of all things, the omelette!

The legend states that Napoleon and his army, traveling through the south of France, stopped overnight near the little town of Bessieres where the local innkeeper made the general an omelette so impressive that Napoleon ordered the townspeople to gather all the eggs in the village to prepare an omelette large enough to feed his entire army. The giant omelette became a tradition to feed the village poor each Easter, and it also became the symbol of a worldwide fraternity rich in friendship, tradition, and cultural exchange called the *Confrerie*.

Member communities in France, New Caledonia, Canada, Belgium, and Argentina send representatives to be knighted as *chevaliers* (chefs) in Abbeville's *Confrerie*, joining under the live oaks of Magdalen Square to chat in French with the locals as they make a giant Cajun omelette.

After the *Maitre de Feu* has scattered sand on the road and arranged wood to light the fire, the ingredients are ceremoniously added under the direction of the Official Ingredients Preparer. Chefs in their tall white hats stir with long wooden paddles to combine more than five thousand eggs in a twelve-foot skillet over the log fire built right in the middle of the street. Every international member has its own unique omelette recipe; Abbeville's features fresh Louisiana crawfish and world-famous Tabasco hot pepper sauce. This popular event, held every November, also features plenty of music and dancing, art shows, house tours, children's activities, and food booths. The Abbeville Giant Omelette Celebration was once even named the Greatest Event on Earth!

For Abbeville, there could be no better celebration. The festival preserves and pays tribute to the very essence of French and Acadian culture—love of family, love of heritage, love of food and fun, and truly the love of life— shared with typical Acadian generosity in a historic setting that remains the very heart of the community.

Bastrop

Population: 11,365

Its origins may be cloaked in mystery and intrigue, but the Main Street commercial community encircling Bastrop's courthouse square stands as an example of what can be accomplished by a dedicated and determined citizenry. In 1785 an Indian trader named Francois Bonaventure began the first settlement in the area, at Point Pleasant on Bayou Bartholomew just outside the present city limits. However, the real colonization effort was due to Baron de Bastrop who in 1796 received a grant of thirty-six square miles from the Spanish governor.

Baron de Bastrop represented himself as a Dutch nobleman fleeing the French Revolution. In reality, Felipe Enrique Neri was born Philip Hendrik Nering Bogel in Dutch Guiana in 1759. Raised in Holland, he married and fathered five children and became a tax collector in the late eighteenth century. Charged with embezzlement and with a reward of one thousand gold ducats on his head, he fled to Spanish Louisiana, adopted the persona of Dutch nobility, and set out to establish a colony in the Ouachita Valley just below what

is now the Arkansas border. After the Louisiana Purchase by the United States, the self-styled baron moved to Spanish Texas, where he acquired a modicum of respectability, engaged in colonization efforts, and represented Anglo-American settlers as an intermediary with the Mexican government.

Large portions of his Louisiana grants were sold to Abraham Morehouse, who in turn sold tracts of this land to some ninety settlers between 1805 and 1813. Cotton and rice began to be cultivated on cleared farmlands, and steamboats began to travel up the Ouachita River. A couple of small stores opened, and a blacksmith named Gillespie created a forge at the crossroads where north-south and east-west travel intersected. It would be at that crossroads that the courthouse for Morehouse Parish would be erected, and this courthouse was a busy place as early settlers tried to secure titles to their lands.

Officially incorporated in the 1850s, the town of Bastrop developed around this 192-acre plot of land purchased by the parish governing body. The courthouse square was the center of both legal and social activity in the early days, and it remains the downtown anchor today, so well loved that in the 1990s the residents of Bastrop approved a tax to completely renovate the 1914 Morehouse Parish Courthouse. The large Beaux Arts structure is noted for beautiful stained glass in its courtroom ceiling beneath the dome, handcrafted wood detail, marble flooring, and decorative plaster and brickwork. The ribbon cutting was

Opposite page: Morehouse Parish Courthouse

held in 2002. Said the Main Street manager, "This massive $5 million total restoration was a monumental achievement, especially when considering that the other option was to tear it down. The downtown was beginning to take shape and civic pride abounded, but Bastrop was fortunate that the downtown never really 'died' out like so many small towns did in the 1970s."

Further improvements were made when outdated aluminum facades, unattractive 1970s "slipcovers," were removed from the commercial structures surrounding the courthouse square, revealing the fine historic brick buildings underneath. "Many younger people had never seen the original buildings or had no recollection of what they looked like," said the Main Street manager. "This project was met with overwhelming support from property and business owners, and as a result all the slipcovers were removed at one time, a feat that has never been matched in Louisiana Main Street history!" Today these commercial structures are filled with thriving businesses, their attractive storefronts shaded by awnings.

In 2000, Bastrop joined the Main Street program, its matching grant funding providing welcome leverage in encouraging millions of dollars in private rehab investment, but the enthusiastic Main Street manager says

there was already a great interest in preserving the city's historical past. "To give proper credit where due," says the manager, "the Rose Theatre was the spark that ignited the fire of restoration. Before the city was a Main Street program, the Rose Theatre was totally restored with strictly volunteers, no federal or state funding, and it stands today as a jewel in the downtown crown." The Rose was built in 1927 to host travelling vaudeville shows and silent movies. Later converted to a movie theater, it closed in the 1970s. In 1985 the Goodwin family donated the property as a community theater and home to a local amateur theater group, the Cotton Country Players. Today the Rose, listed on the National Register of Historic Places and named for

the beloved Goodwin family matriarch, stages dramatic community theater performances, children's workshops, and musical extravaganzas supported by a number of arts and humanities grants. Another historic structure, dating from 1929, houses the Snyder Museum and Creative Arts Center, filled with local artifacts illuminating parish history and heritage.

Downtown amenities followed: attractive parking lots, street furniture, landscaping and lighting, wayfinding signage, banners, and new sidewalks enhance life in the heart of the city. With state and federal assistance, an engaging adaptive re-use project turned a 1930s service station into a visitor center that is now a hub of activity in the historic district. The parish farmers' market downtown was revitalized as well.

Since Bastrop received the Main Street designation, "the organization has never looked back, except to the city's historical past, that is," according to the program manager. Most recently it has cast its eyes upon the 1927 former high school in the historic district with the ambitious goal of restoring it for use as affordable senior housing and filling its halls with aging former students. Listed on the National Register of Historic Places, Bastrop High was also once listed as one of Louisiana's Ten Most Endangered Historic Sites, but a public-private partnership has turned the classrooms and public spaces into sixty-eight independent living units for the elderly, creating jobs and giving residents a sense of place, with continuing education offered in the library. The project promises to attract retirees to help brand Bastrop as a

desirable retirement community, and it stands as a shining example of the possibilities presented by the preservation of historic structures revamped for modern-day viability. "I have not found a group of citizens more committed, effective, or organized in acting together to revitalize their community," said the real estate developer of the nine-year project.

Annual celebrations draw citizens to Bastrop's vibrant historic downtown. Music on Main Street, the concert series on the grounds of the courthouse, and Witch Way to Main Street, the Halloween trick-or-treat children's event sponsored by businesses around the courthouse square, are popular events enhancing Bastrop's sense of community and place. Nearby the Ouachita River and other streams offer great fishing and water sports. Hunting is a favorite fall and winter activity here in Sportsman's Paradise, with its miles and miles . . . and miles . . . of cotton, corn, and soybean fields interspersed with state park and nature preserve properties.

Bastrop has been designated as a Preserve America Community. This national initiative, begun in 2003, recognizes communities that protect and celebrate their heritage, use their historic assets for economic development and community revitalization, and encourage people to experience and appreciate local historic resources through education and heritage tourism programs. This fits right in with the goals of the state and national Main Street programs.

The cooperation of city officials, business owners, and volunteers working together in efforts to develop plans and obtain grant funds serves as an inspiring example for other communities engaged in the struggle to reach a happy balance between preservation and progress. Bastrop Main Street has been so successful that it actually became the subject of a postgraduate dissertation at the University of York in the United Kingdom, compiled by a student with Morehouse Parish ties who found Bastrop Main Street an excellent research subject in the field of historic conservation because it had achieved such success. "Bastrop has done very well considering its size and economic circumstances," said the graduate student in acknowledging the challenges facing the area with the demise of several of its largest employers. "It serves as an example for the international community of what you can do when you have the right leaders."

As Bastrop's Main Steet manager proudly says, "Our crown is filled with all sorts of precious gems—beautiful people, places, and things. We are indeed proud of our tag line of 'Home Town Louisiana' and work every day to live up to the name." This is a community striving to preserve its small-town spirit while building economic and civic growth upon the rock-solid base of its storied past.

Clinton

Population: 1,653

Henry Skipwith was the nephew of Fulwar Skipwith, the distinguished international diplomat who served as Pres. Thomas Jefferson's consul-general to France and then was named head of the government of the Republic of West Florida. Henry obviously travelled in exalted circles, and when he penned his *Sketches of the Pioneers: East Feliciana, Louisiana, Past and Present* as an elderly gentleman, he promised to fill the pages with the history, genealogy, and social characteristics of an area that had attracted as its earliest settlers "a population clinging to the sides of the mountain ranges of the Carolinas and Southwestern Virginia, . . . rugged as the crags and impetuous as the torrents of their native mountains."

And it was a good thing these early settlers to Skipwith's so-called "colony of the Carolinas" were so hardy. According to Skipwith, in 1802 when young Hezekiah Harrell was sent from Charleston to search out a homestead for his family, he labored at clearing the canebrakes along Pretty Creek with a hatchet, but in the dark of night he prudently

retired to sleep in the fork of a tree, "from which secure but uncomfortable roost he would calmly observe the gambols, wrestlings and fights of bears, panthers and wolves." Soon several generations of his family, accompanied by slaves, household goods, and herds of livestock, set out to join him. They traveled by flatboat down the dangerous headwaters of the French Broad and Tennessee rivers, braving the perils of Muscle Shoals with its hidden rocks and strong eddies under the guidance of skilled Indian pilots—often losing a flatboat or two to the dangerous cataracts and whirlpools—thence along the Ohio and Mississippi rivers, and finally overland on foot and by wagon via Natchez, a route followed by many of the early arrivals to the Clinton area.

Another early settler, Eli White, born in 1807, vividly recalled how rustic life was back then. White said,

> I never tasted meat, except bear, venison and an occasional panther steak, until I was a good-sized boy. The only milk I ever tasted was my mother's, until my father returned to South Carolina, and brought out with him one of grandfather's old cows. The dairy utensils my mother used were old-fashioned, big-bellied gourds, sawed in two; my only clothing until I reached twelve years of age was a long shirt of coarse cotton cloth woven on mother's hand loom. I always went barefooted, summer and winter, and my first pair of pants were obtained from mother,

after pleading long and persistently. They were of the fruits of the same old hand loom, made in the old style with broad flap in front, a mile too big in the waist, and couldn't be kept up without suspenders. . . . Our farm in those days was a two-acre patch which we planted in corn and sweet potatoes and cultivated with a little pony and a scooter plow with a wooden shovel board.

And yet Skipwith, writing in 1892, could refer to Clinton as "a widely known and renowned seat of education, social and religious development," and so it was, having in 1824 been designated the seat of government for East Feliciana Parish, its location determined by survey to find the actual center of the parish once divided from neighboring West Feliciana. Commissioners sited the parish seat where Clinton now stands "because it was

well-watered by perennial springs and by Pretty Creek, and wooded by dense forests of pine and hardwoods all around it," according to Skipwith.

John and Susan Bostwick and James Holmes, with architect-constructor George Sebor, acquired the Spanish land grant of Lewis Yarbrough and donated three lots for a courthouse, spring, and jail, then laid out the town of Clinton around them. By the 1820s the village boasted only a scattering of homes plus several saloons and country stores, but within a decade, with the establishment of the Clinton and Port Hudson Railroad connecting the town with the Mississippi River, it had become the center of trading for surrounding cotton plantations. The ensuing prosperity saw a number of handsome homes and commercial structures rising throughout the town. Clinton was officially incorporated in 1852.

Disputes over land boundaries and debt collections soon lured a number of distinguished barristers, called the "flower of the Feliciana bar," into the area. Said Skipwith, "With such a brilliant Society of Intellectual Athletes it is no wonder that churches and schools were the first wants of a community fast growing in refinement and numbers." Soon, he said, "churches went up on every spare lot, and 'old Grocery Row,' a second edition of 'Natchez Under The Hill,' went down."

Education kept step with religious development, with the founding of respected institutes of learning for both boys and girls. Silliman Collegiate Institute for Young Ladies, established in 1852 in handsome brick buildings still used by a private academy today, touted its location

in Clinton as one of the healthiest in the state, its "genial climate and pure atmosphere" enhancing the experience of students being tutored in ancient languages and modern science, vocal music and art, mathematics, mental and moral science, history and composition, English language and literature, and instrumental music.

And as for the "flower of the Feliciana bar," one of their number, Lafayette Saunders, parish judge and state senator who would have been a member of Zachary Taylor's first cabinet had he lived long enough, was obviously a gentleman of many talents, for he built the southernmost building at Silliman and in 1840 also built the magnificent East Feliciana Parish Courthouse. Surrounded by an impressive Doric colonnade and designed by J. S. Savage to replace an earlier courthouse that burned, the two-

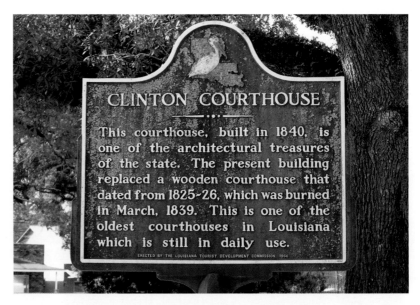

Opposite page: East Feliciana Parish Courthouse

story brick structure stands as one of the South's finest examples of classic Greek Revival architecture.

The full peripteral courthouse, with octagonal cupola towering atop a leaded slate roof, dominates Clinton's public square. On its north side is Lawyers' Row, five Greek Revival buildings of harmonious design, side by side, all dating from the 1840s and 1850s, and several still in their original usage as attorneys' offices. The architectural and historical significance of this amazing group of structures, the courthouse and Lawyers' Row, has been recognized by its designation as a National Historic Landmark, providing a powerful historic document and tribute to the original design and continuous inter-relationships that have served the community well for so long. Even Hollywood has long recognized the striking visual and historical significance of this site, utilizing it as setting for a number of films, including the 1950s classic *The Long Hot Summer* based on William Faulkner's stories and starring Paul Newman, Joanne Woodward, and Orson Welles.

Considered the oldest and arguably the finest courthouse in continuous use in the state, the East Feliciana Parish Courthouse has undergone a lengthy multimillion-dollar restoration and is the crown jewel of Clinton's Historic District and Main Street program. In 2001 the town passed an ordinance that established the Historic District and appointed a commission to oversee changes within the small district as well as other historic properties elsewhere in town wishing to be included. In 2003 Clinton's Main Street program was approved by the state to cover the same area, and the program's façade

grants have provided the means for sprucing up more than a dozen historic structures, including the Audubon Library on Lawyers' Row, the office of the Clerk of Court, the old Clinton High School, and McKnight's, a clothing store.

Since 2006 the program has been aided immeasurably by Friends of Clinton Main Street, Inc., a nonprofit organization established to ensure financial security for the program through fundraisers, grants, and a full-time manager to coordinate the efforts of various parish and town cultural, economic, and historic groups. The focus in Clinton has been not only on preservation but also on developing the arts through shows, workshops, lessons, galleries, and promotion. Clinton's Main Street director

Opposite page: Lawyers' Row

Downtown Clinton

says of the small town with just a couple thousand residents, "We have to make our own entertainment in the country, you know, so we have tried to develop our arts community as well as improve our façades."

The Main Street program here develops and promotes cultural, agricultural, and community events to enhance the popular Clinton Community Market, a fun family-friendly frolic established in the early 1990s with a mere ten vendors that now attracts more than one hundred vendors offering food, music, sidewalk sales, and art exhibits and demonstrations in the Historic District the first Saturday of each month. These regular market days are supplemented by seasonal festivals, with Mardi Gras and Christmas parades, Easter egg hunts, November's

Main to Main Art 'Round The Square, in addition to the Red, White, and Blueberry Festival celebrating the Fourth of July as well as the many productive blueberry farms in the area (there's also a wonderful muscadine winery).

While the Main Street Community and Historic District comprise just a few blocks near the courthouse and make for an easy self-guided walking tour, there are numerous historic structures scattered along the narrow roadways winding up and down the gently rolling hills within Clinton's 2.8 square miles. Woodside, a pleasant Gothic cottage dating from 1847, was occupied by the comptroller of the Clinton Military Academy before it became the home of Judge George Woodside. Stonehenge dates from 1837 and initially housed the family of Judge Lafayette Saunders, builder of Clinton's landmark courthouse. Marston House, a large Greek Revival building, began in 1837 as the Union Bank of New Orleans and later housed the family of the bank cashier who eventually became its president. The Brame-Bennett House, a prime example of Greek temple architecture, was built in 1840. Other interesting early structures include Wedgewood (ca. 1825); Rogers House (early 1800s); Boatner-Record House (ca. 1830); Durham Cottage (ca. 1838); Wall House (ca. 1839); Hope Terrace, built by John Rhea and later used as a girls' school (ca. 1840); Martin Hill (ca. 1840); Durham-Ball House (ca. 1840); Powers-Wheat House (ca. 1845);

Skipwith House (ca. 1850); the George Hays House (ca. 1890); and the Corcoran-DeLee Building, a tenacious survivor of many fires (1836). The Isadore Mayer-Hobgood House, the Kilbourne House, and Wildflower date from around 1900, as does the Brickyard Store, a fascinating mercantile establishment adapted into a residence. Most of these historic structures have helpful identifying signage in the front yards, and tourist information is available at the town hall and at McKnight's downtown.

St. Andrew's Episcopal Church, a small Carpenter Gothic, was built in 1871, and the First Baptist Church dates from the mid-1800s. Clinton also has several cemeteries of great historic interest, including Confederate, Masonic, and Jewish graveyards. The Clinton Confederate Cemetery is a state historic site and the final resting spot of several town founders as well as John Rhea, who founded the Clinton-Port Hudson Railroad and was a leader of the West Florida Rebellion that rid the Florida Parishes of Spanish control in 1810. At the western edge of the cemetery are unmarked graves of hundreds of soldiers killed during the bloody siege of Port Hudson. During the latter years of the Civil War, there were several battles at Clinton, with fierce fighting along Pretty Creek and the railroad line, and the wounded were nursed in the field hospital set up in Marston House, behind which there is another small cemetery.

Clinton today retains indefinable small-town charm, the Main Street historic district seeming to step from another century. Not that it lacks excitement. When *The Dukes of Hazzard* was filmed there, the pace of life picked

up considerably, especially around actress Jessica Simpson in her short-short Daisy Dukes. Clinton also served as Bon Temps, the fictional southern town where telepathic waitress Sookie Stackhouse succumbed to the charms of a vampire in the HBO TV drama *True Blood*. But mostly life just goes on, and a stroll around the courthouse square, taking time to stop and shop and enjoy a few libations along the way, could just as easily be taking place in the nineteenth century as the twenty-first, with people from miles around coming to town to take care of business.

Columbia

Population: 390

The Main Street community in this historic all-American steamboat town is typical in that it wraps around the parish courthouse square, but they say what makes it so different is that it runs right into the Ouachita River. Well, yes. But there's also a fabulously ornate Italian palazzo rising from the sidewalk right on Main Street—from its upper windows the strains of opera would waft in the old days. And there's that iconic little green church nearby, patterned after a Scandinavian house of worship.

Nevertheless, Columbia is the typical early American rivertown. Its scenic waterfront features a monument commemorating the Ouachita River steamboat era, 1819–1927, with tribute lights, benches, and the names of all the old steamboat captains preserved in stone. Concrete steps lead down to the riverside, and the first tier of the overlook is actually the historic foundation of an earlier bridge. The overlook and award-winning scenic riverwalk were developed as part of a Corps of Engineers levee stabilization project after the flood of 1991 caused washouts along the Ouachita's banks, endangering the town.

historic district is lined with tidy brick structures, many of them two stories with decorative trim, housing cafes, restaurants, and small businesses; a favorite gathering spot on Columbia's Main Street is the Columbian Coffee Shop. Columbia is the parish seat of Caldwell Parish, and circling the courthouse square are the expected attorneys' offices, including the former office of the late Louisiana Gov. John J. McKeithen, plus the post office, town hall, school board offices, library, and two banks.

Established in 1827, Columbia's propitious location on the banks of the navigable Ouachita River turned it into a bustling town during the era when the river waters were plied by steamboats. By the onset of the twentieth century, a number of the wooden commercial structures

At the base of the levee on the town side, two other landmarks join the tribute to the steamboat era. The century-old Captain's Quarters, built by or for boat captains, has a boat pilot's wheel gate in its iron fencing and an etching of an old riverboat in its antique entrance door. Formerly called the Ferrand House, this turn-of-the-century structure has been beautifully restored with assistance from Main Street rehab incentive grants and is operated as a bed and breakfast right in the midst of the historic district.

Across Main Street is the Watermark Saloon, infamous as the oldest saloon on the Ouachita and no doubt a welcome sight in the early days as steamboats docked in Columbia to disgorge passengers and freight. There is a watermark showing how high the Ouachita River rose during the devastating 1927 floods. The rest of the

Above: Watermark Saloon

downtown had been destroyed by fires and were replaced with the picturesque brick buildings still standing today.

Many of these small commercial buildings are typical of the times. But remember, there is also among the typical structures a fantastic Renaissance palazzo looking as if it stepped out of fifteenth-century Italy. It seems that many of the early shopkeepers who settled in Columbia were of Italian descent, including John Schepis, a Sicilian architect who arrived in this country nearly penniless, accompanied by his wife and a child born at Ellis Island. In the old country, Signora Schepis had sung grand opera, and her husband was a creative and determined soul as well.

Once in Columbia, they lived in a small borrowed building where they operated a small store. They worked hard and graduated to a larger store. And the dream was born to build a fine showplace that would express their

love not only for the new country but also for the old. In 1916, John Schepis slowly began to assemble this structure himself, painstakingly fashioning the cement building blocks with hollow cores to keep the costs down. From clay he molded two statues to stand guard atop the front façade, making molds of plaster of Paris and then casting them in concrete. These lifesized figures represent George Washington holding an American flag and Christopher Columbus holding an Italian flag; above them flies an American eagle, and in the center is an Italian coat-of-arms.

The statues were laboriously hoisted to the top of the roof with a gin pole, block, and line, and they stand as a loving tribute from a patriotic immigrant to both the country he left behind and the country that allowed him

Above: Close-up of statues
Opposite page: Ouachita River overlook

Above: Columbia Downtown
Opposite page: Schepis Museum

with permanent and rotating exhibits and also provides space for the parish Downtown Development, Chamber of Commerce, and Main Street offices. Columbia's Main Street manager says that the Schepis Museum serves as a centerpiece of the lives of local residents, hosting everything from art and cultural events to board meetings and receptions.

Since Columbia joined the state Main Street program in 1995, many of the downtown structures have been restored, a reclamation process that actually started as a cooperative effort between the town and the Caldwell Parish Industrial Development Board. The success of Columbia Main Street's economic revitalization through historic preservation has won the downtown area several awards, including a coveted "Success Story" award from the state Sea Grant College Program.

Attractions nearby include the First Methodist Church, Columbia's famous "little green church" that is referred to as the town's signature. Built in 1911, it was patterned after a Scandinavian house of worship, with beautiful stained glass windows. The first congregation came together here in the 1840s. The small Meditation Chapel, intended as a place of solitude and quiet prayer, houses religious artwork from around the world, including Gothic chairs from Europe, prayer rails from the Isle of Mann, *prie dieus* from France, American stained glass windows, and a hand-carved head of Christ presented to Gov. John J. McKeithen at the Vatican by Pope John Paul II. On the outskirts of town, the rustic Martin Home Place dates from 1878 and today operates as a living-history

to prosper. Inside this grand Italian opera house, John Schepis located his simple general mercantile store on the ground floor, while the family lived upstairs. Longtime residents recall the Schepis daughter Rosa, a talented musician, flinging open the doors and windows then playing her piano.

Over the years the Schepis Building housed a mercantile store, feed and seed supply, even a skating rink, but by the mid-1970s it was deserted and deteriorating. Listed on the National Register of Historic Places, it was saved by a grant from the Louisiana Division of Historic Places, matched by the Caldwell Parish Industrial Development Board. It has been beautifully restored to serve as a museum

museum, listed on the National Register of Historic Places and offering demonstrations of old-time skills. Also in the vicinity are recreational sites like Dr. Harry Winters' Nature Preserve for birdwatching and hiking trails with labeled plants, the Boeuf Wildlife Management Area for hunting, and a major paleontological and botanical site called Copenhagen Hills, rich in prehistoric fossils and rare plants.

But Columbia's Main Street downtown historic district remains the central focus of life here, and special events attract residents and visitors to enjoy its charms. The Caldwell Country Christmas Parade and Fireworks Display along the river also includes an open house at the Schepis Museum. Witch-Way-to-Main is a children's Halloween celebration, and Mardi Gras on Main involves a children's foot parade and carnival royalty. In October, the decades-old Louisiana Art and Folk Festival is held, with exhibits at the Schepis Museum, art contests, a folkways area with old-time demonstrations, children's activities, and food booths. These fun festivities are sponsored by Columbia Main Street and the Caldwell Parish Chamber of Commerce, and the Lions Club also sponsors a large rodeo in June.

But it's the popular Riverboat Festival in May, featuring

antique cars, live music, arts and crafts, a children's area, and lots of food, that may be the most appropriate celebration here in Columbia. And you get the feeling that if somehow a steamboat from the nineteenth century could dock at the landing today, the captain and passengers would feel right at home. They could wet their whistles at the Watermark Saloon, catch a few winks at the Captain's Quarters, and patronize the bustling little businesses vying for their attention, just as they always did.

Crowley

Population: 13,265

Early settlement patterns in Louisiana followed the major rivers, on fertile high ground built up by centuries of overflow enriching the land and forming natural levees. Once this prime high ground had been claimed, settlers branched out along the smaller bayous and streams, tributaries of the main rivers that provided transportation and rich surrounding lands as well. But those flat, dry treeless prairies in southwestern Louisiana— well, it would take a visionary to see potential there. A visionary and a railroad, too.

Merchant W. W. Duson dabbled in real estate and owned a local newspaper. Where others surveyed the flat, wide-open prairies and saw little prospect, Duson dreamed in the late 1880s of developing a town between Rayne and the Mermentau River. He organized a group of investors into the Southwest Louisiana Land Development Company and purchased 174 acres at forty-five cents an acre. He then enlisted his brother C. C. Duson as partner and used his newspaper to advertise this "garden spot of the world," promising that the lands were rich enough to produce abundant crop yields.

Duson persuaded the recently completed Louisiana Western Railroad (today's Southern Pacific) to move a switch closer to the town site with a promise to name the new town after Pat Crowley, the Irish contractor who graded the railroad roadbed; it was originally known as Crowley Switch. Duson even managed to have his budding community designated the parish seat of government when the area split from St. Landry Parish to become Acadia Parish in 1886. His newspaper proposed the division, and his land company offered property and funding to build a courthouse if Crowley were chosen instead of the nearby commercial center of Rayne. It worked.

The new railroad was vitally important for hauling in lumber and other building materials for the settlement, which by 1890 boasted 240 residents. It would soon grow by leaps and bounds, however, once the railroad ran excursions to recruit new residents. Eager prospects came from across the country, especially the Midwest, where people saw the potential of the prairie for large-scale agricultural ventures.

Acadiana expert Dr. Carl Brasseaux said, "The ready availability of rail service to major national markets, the availability of cheap land, and the region's temperate winters proved irresistibly attractive to thousands of Midwest farmers. . . . After failed attempts to introduce wheat cultivation to the southwestern Louisiana prairies, these Midwestern transplants turned their considerable agricultural skills, ingenuity, and state-of-the-art, steam-powered equipment to the establishment of a major regional rice industry." Gov. Francis T. Nicholls brought

in agronomists to provide expert advice, and the Duson brothers were among the early leaders in establishing the area's rice industry and experimenting with new irrigation and cultivation techniques.

In 1893 Squire Pickett built the first rice mill in Crowley. At one time Crowley milled more rice annually than all of the rice-producing countries in the world combined. Not only did the influx of Midwesterners transform the agricultural and economic base of the area, it also switched the Acadian dietary dependence from corn to rice as the staple starch. Cheap, nutritious, and tasty, rice after the 1920s formed the basis for nearly every Cajun dish and was valued for its ability to stretch a small amount of meat or seafood to feed large families.

Today Crowley is designated the Rice Capital of America, with giant rice mills lining Mill Street and

the Rice Interpretive Center featuring exhibits on the economic impact of the industry on the area. A two-hour driving tour down the Rice Trail passes rice mills to the Rice Experimental Station and crawfish-rice farms like the Crystal Rice Heritage Farm, a working five-generation farm. Indiana wheat farmer Sol Wright, relocating south for health reasons, purchased 320 acres in 1890 for $1,500 and set out to use natural selection and cross-pollination to develop the perfect variety of rice for the Louisiana prairielands. By the 1940s the majority of rice planted in the United States consisted of varieties developed by Wright, and he would be named the first Rice King when Crowley hosted its initial Rice Carnival in 1927.

When Wright died in 1929, the Crowley newspaper commented, "To attempt to set a value upon Sol Wright's contribution to the rice industry and southwest Louisiana

would be like putting a price on the soil, the sunshine or the elements that go into each crop. His monument is renewed each year when the fields turn green, then bend to the harvest." Today the International Rice Festival draws thousands of visitors each October for a full family-fun weekend featuring big-name entertainment, parades, rice royalty, children's day, food booths, arts and crafts, accordion and fiddle contests, a poker run, and a car show. A demonstration of old-time rice threshing augments the rice cooking and rice eating contests, appropriate for this well-established celebration of the harvest.

Laid out in an orderly, one-square-mile grid plan, Crowley was incorporated in 1903 and had six thousand residents by 1917. Many of them prospered sufficiently to

Downtown Crowley

build substantial homes with Midwestern antecedents, still evident in the city's extensive tree-lined forty-block historic district. Quiet residential neighborhoods are full of turn-of-the-century Victorian homes, featuring fascinating Queen Anne and Eastlake architectural influences seen nowhere else in Acadiana in such numbers. Many are listed on the National Register of Historic Places

The jewel of Crowley's downtown Main Street district is the splendid Grand Opera House, built in 1901 by David Lyons, a livery stable owner with big dreams. When built, it provided seating for audiences of more than one thousand in a village that at the time had a total population of only four thousand, but the Opera House packed them in for everything from operatic extravaganzas to personal appearances by Babe Ruth, Buffalo Bill, and

Above: Grand Opera House
Opposite page: Green-Holland House

William Jennings Bryan. Of the "opera houses" that many small towns boasted in the early 1900s, Carl Brasseaux said, "These theaters rarely presented actual operatic productions; instead, they typically hosted 'one-night stands' by traveling troupes of minstrels, vaudevillians, musicians, and journeyman actors . . . complemented by periodic visits by touring circuses and other tent shows and well-attended annual local Chautauquas."

Crowley's Grand Opera House has been beautifully renovated and hosts diverse events and performances. The local Main Street program helps in the rehabbing of historic commercial properties downtown through incentive grants requiring matching private funding, as well as assistance with tax abatement and tax credit programs for restoration projects. The Grand Opera House has been the recipient of several Main Street redevelopment incentive grants during the course of its restoration, as have a number of historic downtown properties since Crowley became a Main Street community in 1999. Working with the local mayor and board of aldermen, Crowley's Main Street program has enthusiastically endorsed its stated mission to recognize, revitalize, and promote the historic, cultural, social, and economic significance of the downtown historic business district and to educate the community about the benefits of its preservation through the involvement of the entire community.

The nearby art-deco Rice Theatre, on the divided downtown boulevard called Parkerson Avenue, is now owned by the city of Crowley. The theater was completed in 1940 and, before it could open its doors, was flooded by a hurricane that inundated the entire area with eight feet of floodwater and drowned upwards of fifty thousand livestock. Thanks to the Rice City Civic Center Restoration Committee, other organizations, and individual preservationists, the theater today hosts a variety of events and activities. The ten-story First National Bank of Crowley building was at one time the tallest between Houston and New Orleans; the bank was founded by W. W. Duson's son-in-law, and there are still some Duson descendants living in the Crowley area today.

W. W. Duson, who looked at the barren prairie and saw the potential for a paradise of bountiful crops and tree-shaded boulevards of beautiful houses, would be proud.

Denham Springs

Population: 10,215

As the name implies, clear-flowing groundwater springs attracted the first settlers to the Denham Springs area, not only as a source of fresh drinking water but also for their healing properties, with mid-nineteenth-century resort hotels attracting ailing guests to partake of the mineral springs' curative powers. The settlement was initially called Amite Springs, then Hill's Springs, and finally Denham Springs for William Denham, who in 1828 purchased some 640 acres and a slave for $1,350 from his father-in-law Alexander Hogue. Hogue and John Noblet had staked the original claims to the land that would become Denham Spring's oldest residential and business districts.

William Denham, who listed his occupation in the 1850 census as farmer, sold the Hogue tract in 1855 to New Orleans businessman Stamaty Covas for just over $3,000. After the Civil War, the same tract went to George L. Minton in 1882 for delinquent taxes, reportedly for a grand total of $124. Minton, a pioneering newspaperman who founded the *Denham Springs News,* subdivided the Hogue-Denham tract and began selling lots for homes

and businesses at about the same time the Noblet tract was being subdivided. Minton also helped start the First Baptist Church and sold property for a four-year boarding school called the Denham Springs Collegiate Institute, which was established in 1895 and enjoyed such a sterling reputation that it attracted students from neighboring communities and teachers from as far away as Virginia.

Incorporated as a village in 1903 with George L. Minton as its first mayor, Denham Springs was proclaimed a town in 1929 and a city in 1957, having grown swiftly once the Baton Rouge, Hammond, and Eastern Railroad (later the Illinois Central) line was completed through town in 1908. The railroad brought increased business and turned the community into a shipping hub for the surrounding truck crop region. With the railroad and improved highways, especially its location at the intersection of Interstate

Hwy. 12 and US 190, Denham Springs became a booming bedroom community for the Baton Rouge metropolitan area. It has attracted major business development, including one of the country's largest Bass Pro Shops stores, not only an outlet for hunting supplies and recreation equipment but, in this area of avid hunters and outdoorsmen, a real tourist attraction as well.

Above and opposite page: Downtown Denham Springs

But right in the heart of town, in the midst of all these bustling modern businesses, lies the quintessential nineteenth-century downtown, lovingly preserved as the Denham Springs Historic Antique District and considered the leading multi-dealer antiques showplace in South Louisiana. In a space of only a few blocks along Range Avenue, there are more than one hundred dealers in dozens of shops and malls, offering an amazing collection of vintage furniture, paintings and pottery, statuary, art and textiles, jewelry, silver and glassware, toys and dolls, books both old and new, and collectibles of every sort, plus gourmet coffee at the Whistle Stop and tasty local cuisine at A Taste of Louisiana Café. Longtime dealers such as Heirlooms by Jo, Heritage House (located in a two-story, century-old boarding house/hotel), Benton Brothers

Antique Mall, Louisiana Purchases, Chandler's Antiques, High Cotton Antiques, Crowder's Antiques, Serendipity in the Village, Seldom Seen Antique Mall, the colorfully named Rusty Rooster, Bee's Knees Children's Boutique, and Baby Cakes draw dedicated customers from around the South to this downtown area of vintage structures offering everything from shabby chic and primitives to exceptionally fine period furnishings.

It was the Carol Theatre that started the comeback of this area, which, like many small downtowns, had become derelict: few functional businesses, little foot traffic, and deteriorating structures. The old theatre was converted into a popular antiques mall and now houses more than thirty booths. Other dealers joined the effort, and Main Street façade grants assisted not only in the rehabbing of Theatre Antiques but also with the restoration of structures housing Heirlooms, Crowder's Antiques, Chandler's Antiques, and Dave's Hardware. Attractive brick paver sidewalks encourage shoppers to stroll along the avenue,

and new parking spaces provide added convenience. The Denham Springs Antique Village has been voted "Best Antiques Shopping" by *Country Roads Magazine* readers, in the top three "Best Louisiana Main Streets" by *Country Roads*, and in the top three "Best Antique Shopping" by readers of AAA's *Southern Traveler* magazine.

The Old City Hall is one of the oldest structures in the Antique Village and now serves as a welcome center, shady pocket park, and museum and repository for historic photos, news articles, local artifacts, and oral history recordings of early residents. It was constructed in the late 1930s under the auspices of the Works Progress Administration and opened to the public in 1940, housing the town hall, town council chambers, police headquarters and jail, courtroom, and a library. It also provided office space for the mayor; prior to its opening, local mayors worked out of their homes.

The police department took over the building when the municipal government outgrew it. Perhaps the most

infamous occupant of the jail's holding cell, according to the Old City Hall curator (whose story is backed up by newspaper accounts of the times), was Mr. Elwood Smith's five hundred-pound, nine-foot-long pet gator named "Sam Smith," which had escaped from its pen and was "arrested" on the Amite River Bridge. Mr. Elwood had to descend from his home on the bluff and drive the errant alligator down the steps and toward home with a stick. Eventually the police moved to a new station, and during the 1990s the Old City Hall, used only for training by the local fire department and as a haunted house at Halloween, deteriorated.

Finally in 1995, Mayor James Delaune established a Historic Preservation Commission, one of whose top priorities was the preservation of Old City Hall. Joining with the Main Street program that was implemented the following year, the commission held events and fundraisers, the city council allocated money, and by 2009 Old City Hall had been restored to its original Art Deco glory, listed on the National Register of Historic Places, and reopened to the public. The Main Street program continued its involvement with the furnishing of the Old City Hall, the lining of the sidewalk at its entrance with commemorative bricks, and the ongoing recording of local history (both oral and visual).

Spring Park preserves one of the springs for which the town was named, while Train Station Park commemorates the importance of the railroad and provides the location for many of the city's special events, summer concerts, Independence Day celebrations, and performances during Antique Village festivals. There are artists' markets and farmers' markets, Mardi Gras and Christmas parades, Pioneer Day with demonstrations of old-time skills, a fun-filled Girls Night Out, and the popular Main Street fundraiser known as Chef's Evening/Wine Tasting in early December when antiques stores stay open late and local restaurants and wine vendors provide samples for hundreds of participants in this old-fashioned community

Christmas celebration. The Antique Village also hosts Spring and Fall Festivals sponsored by the Denham Springs Antique Merchants Association, featuring more than 150 vendors as well as plenty of food, arts and crafts, a pet parade, free children's rides, and live music, and drawing a wonderful mix of locals and visitors to enjoy the old downtown area. Range Avenue is closed to vehicle traffic and is filled with booths for the festivals.

Along with improving the economic outlook, recruiting new businesses, and rehabilitating historic buildings, one of Denham Springs' Main Street program's primary goals is to make downtown a *fun* place to visit. The enormous crowds drawn to the special festivals and events, as well as the daily traffic downtown, are a tribute to the success of the Main Street program here as it strives to improve the competitive position of downtown Denham Springs in relation to other commercial centers, enhance the attractiveness and enjoyment of downtown for shoppers and residents alike, and restore as much of the traditional historic character as possible. This comprehensive process promises to benefit the entire community, not just the downtown area, through economic development and physical improvements.

Does this approach really work? Just ask the hundreds of visitors who flock to the Antique Village for fun-filled days of enjoyable shopping and exciting special-event evenings.

DeRidder

Population: 10,578

Old-timers remembered the world's largest pine tree growing right where DeRidder is located today, but it took the coming of the railroad to connect the area with the rest of the world and make it feasible for lumber companies to begin harvesting the plentiful pine forests and provide the mainstay of local economy. Long before that, as other South Louisiana communities were being founded in the late 1700s and early 1800s, this area was the infamous No Man's Land, a lawless strip of territory along the Sabine River, isolated for years by boundary disputes—first between Spain and France and later between Spanish Texas and the United States. No traveler in his right mind, it was said, would cross this territory without armed companions; only a few brave squatters settled there, and even fewer lived to tell the tale.

The boundary dispute was finally settled in 1819, but it was not until 1893 that, a dozen miles east of the Sabine River border with Texas, Calvin Shirley built the first house in DeRidder. It was constructed of puncheons (split log slabs with a smooth face) covered with hand-rived board shingles, on 160 acres that would later be platted as the original DeRidder town site. Within a few years the Pittsburgh & Gulf Railroad (later the Kansas City Southern), laying track from Kansas City to Port Arthur, used the town site as a camping spot for the railroad workers; as soon as acreage was purchased from Calvin Shirley, a ramble of rude shacks was hastily constructed.

By the time the railroad was up and running in 1898, DeRidder was home to some three hundred residents, a sawmill, a hotel, and some small stores as well. But as early pioneer Eva Stewart Frazar recalled, "This section was 50 years behind the rest of the world. It was not the fault of the people who lived here. It was the fact that they had such poor contact with the outside world, because there were no roads."

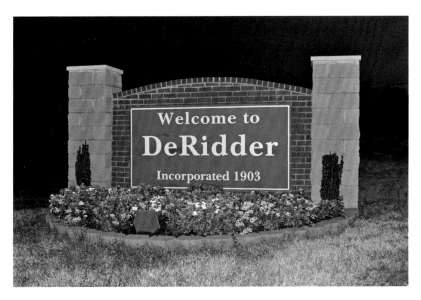

It wouldn't take long for it to catch up, however, for DeRidder was surrounded by nearly 700,000 acres of virgin forest, mostly longleaf pine, which quickly attracted lumber companies with droves of loggers and sawmill workers. DeRidder was incorporated as a town in 1903, and the next several decades were boom years. It was not until 1927 that the last large mill closed, and it would be a couple of decades after that before any serious reforestation attempts would be made.

In 1912 DeRidder was certified as the parish seat of Beauregard Parish, named for Louisiana's illustrious Confederate Gen. Pierre Gustave Toutant Beauregard. Col. William Louis Stevens, renowned New Orleans institutional architect, was engaged to design an imposing courthouse and, next door, a jail. The two structures were connected by an underground tunnel but separated by centuries in style. The 1914 courthouse, an opulent Beaux Arts style with colossal coupled columns at the entrance loggias, is topped by a large dome with a clock face on each side. Of buff brick with white-glazed terra cotta and stone trim, the courthouse has an octagonal lobby and reaches an impressive height of six stories at the apex of the dome. This is Beauregard Parish's largest structure and its first and only courthouse, still in use and listed on the National Register of Historic Places. For criminals convicted in the two-story courtroom inside this elegant courthouse, being transported to the dark Gothic jail next door must have seemed like stepping into a horror movie, especially after 1928 when it became infamous as the "hanging jail" after two murderers were strung up from the barred grate above

the three-story spiral staircase. With blasted concrete walls thirteen to twenty-one inches thick, the hulking structure is described as the "collegiate Gothic" style more popular for universities and churches, with arches, a central tower, barred dormer windows upstairs, and quarters for the jailer and his family on the first floor.

The jail has not been in use since the 1980s (it is now undergoing asbestos removal to prepare it for future use), but the courthouse square remains the focal point of historic downtown DeRidder, a district of more than forty structures significant enough to be listed on the National Register of Historic Places. The Old Post Office, across from the courthouse, has a large colorful fresco called "Rural Free Delivery," completed in 1936 by Conrad Albrizio, whose murals were commissioned for post offices around the South by the WPA during the Depression.

Above: Beauregard Museum
Opposite page: Beauregard Parish Courthouse (left) and jail (right)

The Beauregard Museum has interesting exhibits on DeRidder's formative years and shares space with the Lois Loftin Doll Museum in the old 1927 Depot, paying tribute to the days when bustling DeRidder had four railroads and ten passenger trains per day. Parked by the Depot is a stainless steel caboose from the sixties. Visitors here come to appreciate how much the town owed the railroad, including even its name, reportedly bestowed by a Dutch railroad financier whose sister-in-law was the lovely Ella de Ridder. When railroad founder Arthur Stilwell ran short of funds to complete his track from Kansas City to the Gulf because of an international financial crisis in 1893, he sought and received some $3 million in assistance collected by an acquaintance in Amsterdam, a young coffee merchant named Jan Dehouyen or DeGoeijen, who subsequently joined the railroad company and provided the name for several stops along the line— Vandervoort for his mother's maiden name; Mena, Arkansas, for his wife; and DeRidder for his favorite sister-in-law, the beautiful and artistic Ella. Dehouyen's son John visited DeRidder in 1973 as an elderly man and presented the city with a picture of his aunt.

The picturesque structures in the commercial district lining the

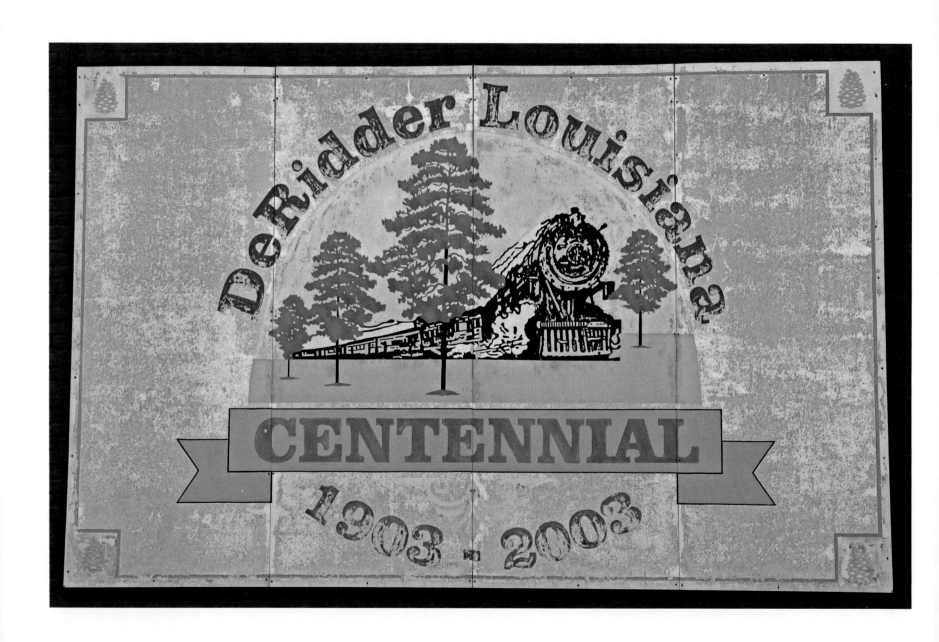

railroad tracks downtown were primarily built after April 1904 when an early morning fire destroyed most of the business section of DeRidder, including every building from the corner of Washington Avenue and West First Street north of Washington to the corner of North Washington and Shirley Street. One George Smith, described as a gambler, was indicted for arson by a grand jury. "The man reportedly left town," summarily said accounts of the times.

The lumber industry experienced a decline after cutting much of the local pine. The stumps left behind were dynamited and turpentine was extracted to fuel another local industry. Then the military came to town. Central Louisiana would be the site of the largest peacetime military maneuvers ever—covering more than 300,000 square miles in the summer of 1941—as the United States prepared for World War II. Nearly half a million soldiers and a distinguished command staff came

together to devise strategy and practice tactics that would eventually contribute to Allied victory by mechanizing forces, field testing new equipment, and training fresh troops in war games. The training camps, airfields, and other installations built for these maneuvers would shape the course of history in this area.

Local historians recall that the "mix of saloons and soldiers during the Louisiana Maneuvers led to streams of convoys on roads, horse cavalry on streets, brawling in downtown DeRidder and bivouacs on farms." The excitement no doubt contributed to the fact that Beauregard Parish was dry for many years (a rarity so close to South Louisiana's Cajun *joie de vivre*), although the town of DeRidder is no longer. But this also led to the establishment of one of the country's first United Service Organizations, providing off-base socialization

and recreational opportunities for thousands of young soldiers far from home, some of whom would later become famed military leaders. In November 1941, the DeRidder USO opened as one of the first five designated structures built with federal funding to offer servicemen space for showers, meals, movies, and thrice-weekly dances in what is now known as the War Memorial Civic Center in the south end of DeRidder.

Folks still flock to historic downtown DeRidder, where banners proclaim "Shop, Dine, Discover DeRidder." Downtown at Sundown, hosted by the city, offers spring and fall concerts in the Amerisafe Pavilion; the Wooten Theatre's community players and Realart DeRidder's cooperative art gallery have sparked a cultural revival; and in the spring the Arts Parade concert series offers live music sponsored by the city and Impromptu Players. Major festivals include the Louisiana Doll Festival, the Watermelon Festival, La Cuisine de Beauregard Food Festival, Fourth of July Fireworks, SWLA All Veteran's Reunion, and a Christmas Festival called Miracle on Washington Street, complete with Chamber of Commerce parade and many seasonal shopping opportunities. The annual Beauregard Parish Fair brings crowds to DeRidder in the fall with another parade, plus food, music, and fun, and there are other festivals dedicated to the celebration of yo-yos, gems and minerals, Native American culture, and mudbugs, as well as weekend trade days.

This area is known for its recreational opportunities, with a number of lakes offering boating and exceptional fishing, plus camping and wilderness hiking through the piney hills in the nearby Kisatchie National Forest, Louisiana's only national forest. Also in the area is a thriving Mennonite community first settled in the 1930s, when promotional literature published by the Longbell Lumber Company attracted a group of farmers whose Kansas homesteads were being ravaged by severe dust storms.

DeRidder is one of the newer Main Street communities, having joined the program in 2008, but it is already making an impact with grants and encouragement aimed at revitalizing the town's historic downtown district.

Donaldsonville

Population: 7,436

Native Americans established a village here, recognizing the virtues of this site at the confluence of the Mississippi River and Bayou Lafourche, which was itself one of the prehistoric main channels of the river and was referred to by La Salle and early European explorers as *La Fourche des Chetimaches*. Beginning as a trading post around 1750, Donaldsonville would be the third town incorporated in Louisiana, founded in 1806 by William Donaldson on the farm of Pierre Landry, with plans drawn by Barthélémy Lafon featuring lots laid out in grids and several grand public spaces—notably, Louisiana Square and the semicircular space called Crescent Park along the Mississippi—designed to welcome river traffic.

As the jumping-off point for all traffic and trade going down the bayou, Donaldsonville soon developed into a bustling community at the center of the second Acadian coast, the economic and cultural hub of the region. In 1811, it was the only post office in the 190-mile stretch between New Orleans and Pinckneyville in the Mississippi Territory, and it served as Louisiana's state capital from January 1830 to January 1831—only a single year because the legislators found it too boring and insisted on moving back to New Orleans. By the 1840s, residents of Donaldsonville could travel across the river via a hand-powered ferry that "by laborious effort for nearly an hour" was capable of crossing the Mississippi with a skiff affixed to each side of a barge. Charges were twenty-five cents for foot passengers and two dollars for gig and horse. The town boasted fifty stores supplying the needs of townsfolk and the surrounding sugarcane plantations, as well as several banks, a theater, and a hospital.

As the Civil War brought turmoil and tragedy to the region, Donaldsonville found that its location between river and bayou mouth would prove not only a blessing but also a curse. In 1862 Confederate cavalry operating near Donaldsonville continually fired upon and harassed Union ships on the Mississippi. Admiral David Farragut threatened that if the sniping did not cease, he would bombard Donaldsonville, which the Federals called "the piratical resort of all the bad men of the country." When the harassment continued, Farragut obliterated the town, first with shelling from several gunboats and then by landing a party of Union troops who burned what was left standing. Over two-thirds of the town was demolished, reducing it to "a desert of smoke-blackened ruins, nearly all in ashes."

Federal troops then constructed a star-shaped earthen fort surrounded by an impassable open moat sixteen feet wide and twelve feet deep on the west bank of Bayou Lafourche close to the river. It was named for Gen. Benjamin Butler, Union occupier of New Orleans, and in June 1863 it would become one of the first battle locations marked by the valiant participation of black troops, who previously had found themselves relegated to building bridges, digging ditches, and other menial labor as if they were still slaves instead of soldiers. A monument at the site of Fort Butler commemorates the contributions of these troops, many of them convalescents recovering from fighting at the Siege of Port Hudson up the river, as they repulsed Confederate cavalry attacks with heavy firepower support from Federal gunboats on the river. Casualties among cavalrymen, most of them Texas Rangers, who tried to cross the open moat and scale fort walls were so heavy that one observer wrote after the battle was over that "the sun rose upon a ghastly sight, upon green slopes gray with the dead, the dying and the maimed, and the black ditch red with their blood."

But within a decade Donaldsonville, governmental seat of Ascension Parish, was bouncing back. A steam ferry called the *Little Minnie*, with an 8 hp motor and an upstream speed of 8 mph, crossed the Mississippi, accommodating horses and buggies or carriages on the steamboat itself, with an attached flatboat for larger wagons, mules, and stock. The New Orleans, Mobile, and Chattanooga Railroad made Donaldsonville its western terminus in the 1870s, with a horse-powered turntable built to reverse the train on the track. The road through town to the depot became a beautiful commercial corridor, a great improvement from the days when local streets were in such bad condition after heavy rains that the newspaper editor wrote he'd rather stick a nail in his foot than walk to the train station after a downpour; in 1895 the local governing body had adopted an ordinance requiring wagons and carts to drive in zig-zag fashion to minimize ruts.

One impressive structure built in 1877 on Railroad Avenue was the B. Lemann & Bro. Building, constructed by Bernard and Myer Lemann to house the mercantile business started by their father Jacob in 1836. Designed by noted New Orleans architect James Freret in the ornate Italianate style popular at the time, the 60,000-square-foot stuccoed brick building has a colonnade of fluted cast-iron columns supporting an overhanging gallery on three sides. At one time, it was the oldest continuously operated family-owned department store in the state, proffering groceries both retail and wholesale, men's and ladies' clothing, piece goods, notions, and hardware. When Jacob Lemann died in 1887, the newspaper obituary referred to

him as one of the largest planters and property holders in Ascension Parish and a man of honor and integrity.

The Lemanns were among a sizable population of Jewish immigrants whose business skills were vital for facilitating Donaldsonville's recovery in the days after the Civil War. Escaping religious persecution and economic oppression in Europe and often arriving in this country penniless to begin working as pushcart peddlers, they settled along major river trade routes and thrived not

Italianate B. Lemann & Bro. Building

River Road African-American Museum

only economically but also socially and politically. By the 1870s, Donaldsonville had more than seventy families worshipping in its synagogue, and the 1856 Bikur Sholim Cemetery had more than 120 graves. The town has had more Jewish mayors than any other in the South.

The Lemann Building has housed the Historic Donaldsonville Museum with exhibits on local history. Nearby, the River Road African-American Museum focuses on the contributions of antebellum slaves and free persons of color, including Pierre Caliste Landry (1841–1921), a former slave who became the nation's first black mayor when elected in 1868. A lawyer, educator, and ordained minister, Landry later served in the state legislature and also founded St. Peter's Methodist Church.

The Ascension Parish Courthouse and Louisiana

Ascension Parish Courthouse

Square were placed on the National Register of Historic Places in 1979. The present brick courthouse, designed in 1889 by Freret, is exuberantly Romanesque Revival, with a central clock tower and arched windows and door openings. In 1848, the original State House, where the legislature met during Donaldsonville's brief tenure as state capital in 1830, was razed and its bricks used to curb erosion at the mouth of Bayou Lafourche.

A large National Register Historic District was established in Donaldsonville in 1984 and includes more than six hundred significant structures, both great and small, commercial and residential, most of them dating from just after the Civil War as the determined town rose from the ashes. This beautiful area, more than fifty blocks, is one of the state's most extensive historic districts and is considered the finest collection of significant vintage structures in any of the Mississippi River parishes above New Orleans. The commercial corridor of Railroad Avenue has a wonderful assortment of late nineteenth- or early twentieth-century structures housing antique shops, bed and breakfasts, restaurants, art galleries, and other viable businesses; among varied architectural styles are false-front and provincial Italianate buildings, plus several neoclassical and Romanesque Revival structures. Parallel to Railroad Avenue runs Lessard Street, which boasts rows of large, impressive Victorian homes at the river end and rows of small shotgun houses decked out with gingerbread trim at the other.

The beautiful Ascension Catholic Church was founded in 1772 as *La Iglesia de la Ascension de Nostro Senor Jesu*

Downtown Donaldsonville

Cristo da Lafourche de los Chetimaches by Father Angel de Revillagodos on orders of King Charles III of Spain. The present Gothic structure dates from the late 1870s. At the time the church was established, the Lafourche district had more than 350 residents, which the Spanish government agreed was sufficient to support a church parish. The church served as civil and social center, with legal business such as land sales conducted at the church door after mass and government documents posted on the church doors. In 1845 the church donated lands for the Sisters of Charity of St. Joseph from Maryland to open a convent and small school, where they stirred up controversy by teaching English instead of the French customary to the area.

Since joining the state program in 2008, Donaldsonville Main Street, with assistance from an army of dedicated volunteers and the many artists and craftsmen involved in the recently approved Cultural District, has shown great enthusiasm for the revitalization of downtown. In the face of tightened belts and painful budget cuts, they are not averse to manning paint brushes and brooms to spruce up the many fine structures that make this such a picturesque commercial area. Events sponsored by Main Street and the Downtown Development group include Third of July Fireworks on the Levee; an Avenue Evening Stroll in November as part of statewide Main to Main celebrations with wandering musicians, horse-drawn buggies, merchants, and artists; and Stash the Trash clean-up projects in April. An especially popular late spring event, Cruisin' the Avenue brings classic cars and car enthusiasts downtown.

There's a scenic walkway atop the Mississippi River levee as well as a welcoming tree-shaded park; throw in plenty of good food, live music, and entertainment, and these events are sure to bring hordes of participants downtown to enjoy the atmosphere and patronize the businesses. And that's what Main Street Donaldsonville is all about, preserving the history and vintage buildings in sustainable and profitable ways that the residents and visitors of today and even tomorrow can appreciate and enjoy.

Opposite page: Ascension Catholic Church

Eunice

Population: 10,398

They all landed as exiles in Louisiana in the late 1700s. They shared the same traumatic background, the same French language, and much of the same culture. Yet miles separated the Wetlands Acadians from the Prairie Cajuns. Life in the flat dry prairielands of southwestern Louisiana was a far cry from life in the bayous, swamps, and coastal marshes, and nowhere can one gain a clearer understanding of the differences than in Eunice, which calls itself Louisiana's Prairie Cajun Capital.

Pioneer land developer, rice farmer, state senator, and legendary Louisiana lawman C. C. Duson (his name was Cornelius but folks called him Curley) had helped his brother W. W. found the railroad switch town of Crowley in the 1880s, when C. C. was sheriff of St. Landry Parish. He had a widespread reputation for fearlessly pursuing escapees and for being a crack shot, once killing ninety-six alligators with ninety-six shots. In 1906 Pres. Theodore Roosevelt appointed him U.S. Marshal for the Western District of Louisiana.

After he helped establish Crowley and ended his career as sheriff, C. C. Duson cast his eyes upon the wide-open prairielands to the north and determined to develop a separate town named for his young second wife, Eunice Pharr Duson. In 1894 he purchased 160 acres of prairie, divided it into lots with a broad boulevard running through the center and east-west side streets named for trees (and landscaped with the appropriate tree specimens), and convinced the Southern Pacific railroad to extend its line there. His enthusiastic newspaper advertisements attracted several trainloads of prospective buyers to a day-long auction, complete with a feast, *fais do do*, and free train ride; some 150 lots were sold at approximately $100 apiece. Today Eunice finds itself in two different parishes, a small portion of the southern part of town in Acadia Parish, the majority in St. Landry. A bronze statue of Eunice Pharr Duson holding a bouquet of prairie wildflowers presides over the historic district, and the old train depot from which these first land sales were made now houses a museum with exhibits on early life here.

An even more complete explication of pioneering experiences in the area may be found at the Prairie Acadian Cultural Center unit of the Jean Lafitte National Park and Preserve, located on that early boulevard called Park Avenue. Here artifacts and live demonstrations interpret the rich culture of the Acadians who settled in different circumstances from their counterparts along the Mississippi River and other waterways and wetlands. Beginning in the 1760s, the first Acadian exiles spread out beyond the Atchafalaya Basin and onto the vast southwest

prairies from the trading posts at Opelousas and Attakapas (St. Martinville). At first they thought the prairies were only good for cattle to range and outlaws to hide; the switch grass and broom sedge grew six feet tall and colorful wildflowers brightened the wide expanses, broken only by lines of trees growing along the few small bayous and coulees. Semi-wild longhorn herds ranged on unfenced prairie, and communal roundups were accomplished in the Acadian *coup de main* (lend a hand) tradition, just as were the housewarmings and *boucheries* (pig butchering), where family and neighbors joined in to help get the job done.

The introduction of new crops and the coming of the railroad expanded the possibilities of the prairielands for agricultural ventures, and they proved so perfect for the cultivation of rice that soon there were few stretches of virgin prairie left (ten acres of restored ecosystem have been preserved at the Eunice Cajun Prairie Site). Early settlements hugged the bayous, but once the railroad opened up the prairie interiors, a string of railroad towns

Above: Statue of Eunice Pharr Duson

sprang up, stitched together by the tracks of *le chemin de fer*. Visitors to the Prairie Acadian Cultural Center learn about early life in the Eunice area as these Acadian immigrants adapted their old ways to a new world, explained not just through exhibits but through the unique opportunity to interact with skilled local musicians and craftspersons and assorted Cajun characters giving hands-on demonstrations while sharing their appreciation of what real Acadian enjoyment of life is all about.

An even greater appreciation for that famous Cajun *joie de vivre* is provided every Saturday night at Eunice's historic Liberty Theater. This is not a tourist demo, folks, this is

real life. Locals flock in to dance to live music in a restored 1924 vaudeville/movie house that during its heyday in the 1920s and '30s was called southwest Louisiana's "Premier Temple of Amusement," hosting such stellar personalities as Fatty Arbuckle and Roy Rogers and the Bowery Boys along with operas, plays, and vaudeville performances. This is a continuation of the *bals de maison* (house dances) tradition, another important social institution that ensured group cohesiveness. In the early days, these neighborhood folk dances provided welcome respite from the daily grind of backbreaking work while preserving the traditional culture of the Acadians—the music, dancing, language, and cuisine. Neighbors took turns hosting the dances, and Saturday nights found the yards crowded with horse-drawn vehicles and mule carts parked under

chinaberry trees and hitched to picket fences. Old men played cards in a corner, babies were put to sleep, and on the dance floor (which might be the gallery, the main room cleared of its meager furnishings, or even the farmstead's dirt yard), cotillions and round dances were performed with exceptional grace to the strains of a fiddle. In the early twentieth century these dances moved from rural homesteads to dance halls.

Today, at the Liberty Theater, the Saturday night *Rendez-vous des Cajuns* show features the best of live Cajun and Zydeco music, broadcast in French on radio and television. The dance floor below the stage fills with multigenerational dancers aged from two to ninety-two, the wrinkled and sunburned old men in their cowboy hats and the ladies all gussied up, local regulars whose graceful dexterity on the dance floor transcends age and warms the heart as they converse in French and tolerate the occasional tourist galloping clumsily around the floor. Other popular Eunice venues for music lovers are the Cajun Music Hall of Fame and Museum, housed in a former one-room country store, the Savoy Music Center, where famed musicians Marc and Ann Savoy host jam sessions, and Nick's on 2nd dance hall.

The Liberty Center for the Performing Arts, as it has been called since it became the property of the city and was beautifully restored during the administration of former Mayor Curtis Joubert, adds extra performances for Eunice's huge Mardi Gras celebration, which features four full days of jam sessions, street dances, old-time *boucheries*, demonstrations at the Prairie Acadian Cultural

Ardoin's Department Store on Second Street

Courir de Mardi Gras Participants

in excitable horses ridden at breakneck speed, accordions and fiddles, and plenty of beer, and it's no wonder when the hosts toss live chickens into the air hilarious mayhem ensues.

Other annual events in Eunice include the World Championship Crawfish Étouffée Cook-off, the Cajun Music Festival, holiday activities around Christmas and the Fourth of July, a Farmers' Market sponsored in season by Main Street, as well as Main to Main activities in November. Most activities center around Eunice's historic downtown area, along Second and Third streets, Park Avenue, Walnut Street, and C. C. Duson Drive. Once Eunice became a Main Street community in 1999, rehab grants assisted in the restoration of downtown commercial structures like the Queen Cinema. Opened in 1937 by the owners of the Liberty Theater, it was rebuilt around a Quonset hut after a fire in 1946 and completely renovated

Center, and children's activities. But the main feature is the traditional rural *Courir de Mardi Gras* with a cast of hundreds of masked participants both male and female, mounted on horses and flatbeds, in wildly flamboyant costumes. And if you've ever been to Mardi Gras in New Orleans or Mobile or any of the other urban sites and think you've seen it all, you ain't seen nothin' yet! In gaudy costumes mocking the ancient nobility and other authority figures, mounted participants roam the rural countryside, stopping at designated houses to dance and entertain and cavort until the homeowner donates ingredients for a communal gumbo to be served at the *fais do-do* when the riders return to town—dirty, disheveled, and more than a few of them dead drunk. This last raucous revelry before the austerity of Lent in these small rural Catholic Cajun communities has its roots in medieval times; throw

beginning in 2009. Other Second Street historic sites in this little jewel of a commercial downtown district include the Ardoin department store building which housed Eunice's first Cajun dancehall on its second floor; the Louis Wright Store, founded in 1911; Café Mosaic coffeehouse; Nicks on 2nd, opened in 1937 as a men's bourré club with alcoholic refreshments stashed on the second floor during Prohibition; and a wonderful mural by internationally acclaimed artist Robert Dafford, who also created the Liberty Theater's stage backdrop.

Dafford's mural shows the Cajun prairie, and Eunice, as the capital of the Cajun prairie, remains proud of its heritage. Its Main Street program joins other community efforts committed to preserving the traditions and culture of those prairie Cajuns. This is a community with an enduring sense of place and a determination to continue to celebrate its culture through the preservation of historic structures and historic practices, all to the accompaniment of traditional music, feasting, and dancing and the sheer enjoyment of even the most mundane aspects of daily living.

Franklin

Population: 7,660

Franklin is a little island of English culture adrift in a sea of French, Creole, and Acadian, like the crowning dollop of meringue afloat on the custard base of a fancy old-fashioned Floating Island dessert. One end of its Main Street is lined with picturesque commercial structures, the other with immense white-columned mansions, some dating from the 1820s and 1830s, shaded by ancient live oaks. The median ground of the broad boulevard running through this section (East Main Street, Hwy. 182), surely one of the loveliest downtown residential areas in the state, is lined with iconic Victorian light standards, their bases stamped "Do not hitch" to deter errant carriage drivers or mounted loiterers. Indeed, town ordinance number 185, passed in May 1916, forbade not only the hitching of horses or wagons to the lampposts, but also banned delinquent loose chickens from the neutral ground.

Founded in 1808 on the Old Spanish Trail along picturesque Bayou Teche, Franklin became the seat of St. Mary Parish in 1811. Originally called Carlin's Settlement, it was

renamed for Benjamin Franklin and developed into an important inland port with the advent of sternwheeler steamboat traffic. The bayou, lined with so many fine plantation homes that it was called "the main street of Acadiana," enabled the planters living along its banks to easily ship their sugar and molasses to markets in New Orleans and points beyond. From the ranks of these wealthy planters came an astounding number of early statesmen: five state governors and a lieutenant governor, four United States senators, and a chief justice of the state Supreme Court.

The storied mansions of these old families bespeak a cultured lifestyle on the productive sugar plantations lining the magical, meandering Teche. In the 1830s, Bayside Plantation's Francis DuBose Richardson, sugar

planter and newspaper correspondent, observed the unique culture surrounding him. The Creole population of southwest Louisiana, by which he meant all the early plantation families, regardless of national ancestry, "represented the wealth and power of their section. The planters generally had an easy time of it; very few of them in debt, they fared sumptuously every day . . . moved about in good style and equipage . . . polished people; after the similitude of their ancestry, jealous and sensitive of their honor and brave in defending it." Their gatherings were marked with "genteel hilarity; *bon vivants* they were who enjoyed the good things of this world."

The Franklin area today joyfully maintains that heritage, that same *joie de vivre,* the enjoyment of life in this tropical setting along the storied bayou lined with ancient live oaks whose branches reach down to caress the brown waters. Louisiana author Harnett T. Kane called the serene Teche "the Past in Louisiana," its lush setting fertilizing a lifestyle not quite that of rural places nor yet that of cities, comparable to that of the Russian provinces of czarist times, days of "heavy magnificence in distant reaches." The curving passages of the bayou gave rise to its Chitimacha Indian name Teche, its twists and turns said to have been caused by the writhings and death throes of a great snake killed by the arrows and clubs of one thousand brave warriors.

The Grevemberg House Museum, salvaged by the St. Mary Landmarks Society, gives visitors a good picture of life in the nineteenth century here, for it has been meticulously restored and beautifully furnished with exqui-

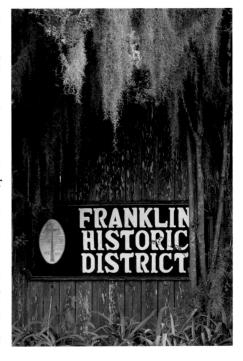

site period pieces and portraits. The double-galleried Grevemberg House is an outstanding example of Greek Revival architecture. The townhouse was built in 1851 for the widow and children of Albania Plantation's Gabriel Grevemberg, who was one of hundreds who drowned in the 1856 hurricane that wiped out the popular Victorian resort on Isle Dernier off the Louisiana coast. Another architectural treasure in Franklin is St. Mary's Episcopal Church, established in 1830 by the state's fourth-oldest Episcopal congregation. When the original structure burned in 1870, it was quickly rebuilt as one of the finest examples of mid-nineteenth-century Carpenter Gothic church architecture in the South. Franklin's First United Methodist Church was established in 1806 as the state's first Protestant church. The Roman Catholic Church of the Assumption has grand stained glass windows.

Today the entire Franklin Historic District is listed on the National Register of Historic Places and contains more than 420 significant structures, not only in the

original mid-nineteenth-century neighborhood along the Teche but also in the more densely packed railroad town dating from later in the century. Street names commemorate respected old families—among them Palfreys, Cafferys, Trowbridges, and Fosters. The latter provided not one but two state governors, both Murphy J. Fosters, grandfather and grandson. Former governor Mike Foster's home, glorious Greek Revival Oaklawn Manor, on Bayou Teche at Irish Bend near Franklin, dates from 1837 and is open for tours.

Confederate Gen. Richard Taylor, whose outnumbered troops at the 1863 Battle of Irish Bend caused so many Federal casualties as to help prevent an invasion of Texas, said of the Teche country, "In all my wanderings, and they have been many and wide, I cannot recall so fair, so bountiful, and so happy a land." More recently Franklin was Louisiana's only town included in Norman Crampton's *The 100 Best Small Towns in America*, and it has repeatedly won the award as Louisiana's Cleanest City.

The commercial corridor of Franklin's Main Street is a bustling area full of historic charm and character, alive with activity and punctuated with multi-story masonry structures with stepped gables, arched windows, pilasters, crenellations, and corbelled brickwork. There are no errant chickens scratching in the median here, nor horses hitched to the lampposts. Specialty shops, business offices, and restaurants offering Cajun and Creole dishes stay busy, and the inviting walkways along Bayou Teche provide close-up views of the tranquil waterway. For more extensive observations, the Bayou Teche Scenic Byway

Above and opposite page: Downtown Franklin

traces the bayou for 125 miles between Patterson and Port Barre.

Downtown Franklin is headquarters for the Bayou Teche Black Bear and Birding Festival every April. This popular festival features hiking and canoe trips through the 9,000-acre Bayou Teche National Wildlife Refuge, birding forays to view the many migratory birds passing through, fireworks, great food, live music, beauty pageants, the "Running of the Bears" 5-K run/walk, arts and crafts, educational exhibits, the "Tour de Bear" bike tour, teen and children's activities like a teddy bear repair clinic, and a wooden boat display. Even pets get into the act with a Mutt Strutt and "Who's Ya Daddy Ugly Dog Contest." Something for everybody, you might say, but the main mission of the festival is to promote ecotourism and provide education about the endangered Louisiana black bear, a threatened species traditionally found in abundance in the area.

Another popular Franklin get-together is October's Harvest Moon Festival, which encourages downtown shopping and support for local merchants. Sponsored by the Franklin Merchants Association, this is a celebration of the cane farming culture and the hard work that culminated in the bountiful harvests for which Franklin area sugar plantations were noted. In August, the annual Art Walk, *Promenade d'art de Franklin*, is sponsored by the Main Street program and St. Mary Parish Chamber of Commerce and hosted by local merchants to draw art enthusiasts clad in white linen downtown to view exhibits and meet participating visual artists. Franklin Main Street also chooses the "Lamplighter" who ceremoniously turns on the Christmas lights each year, a prestigious position recognizing a resident whose good deeds and community spirit extends beyond the holiday season.

Since becoming a Main Street community in 1984, Franklin has benefitted from numerous rehab incentive grants encouraging matching private investment in its historic downtown commercial community, with dozens of new businesses established and close to two hundred new jobs created. Working closely with St. Mary Parish's Economic Development program, the Chamber of Commerce, and the very active Cajun Coast Visitors and Convention Bureau, Franklin's Main Street program assists in tourism promotion, special event planning, and the revitalization of the downtown district.

One Main Street redevelopment incentive grant provided funding to assist in the reclaiming of a turn-of-the-century wooden structure on Main Street that is called the Lamp Post. Now providing much-needed rental space for events, the building was in deplorable condition until new owners, with the long-term vision to adapt it for present-day community benefit, overcame nearly insurmountable odds to turn it into what the Main Street director calls the colorful "crown jewel" of the commercial district. The project exemplifies Franklin Main Street's aim of making a revitalized downtown viable and fun, building on its inherent assets like rich architecture, personal service, traditional values, and strong sense of place.

And if there is anywhere that has a great sense of place, it is Franklin.

Hammond

Population: 20,019

Railroad town, college town, and early strawberry capital—where perfect berries were grown in such profusion that special trains called the Crimson Flyers transported the fruit to northern markets—Hammond means many different things to its more than 20,000 residents. But there's one thing upon which they all agree—they *love* their historic downtown. They live there, dine there, shop there, do business there, and party there. In fact, the main thing the city's Comprehensive Master Plan reveals is that they wouldn't change a thing about it, except to preserve it and enhance its historic character. According to the residents of Hammond, their extensive downtown area contains what is best about the city, exemplifying the unique community character and proud heritage of one of the largest of Louisiana's Main Street communities.

Beloved Congressman James H. Morrison, who represented the area in Washington for many years, saw to it that when the interstate highway system was developed in the 1950s, the routes of Interstate Hwys. 55 and 12 intersected right at his historic hometown, bringing

booming business, shopping malls, and big-box stores to the outskirts of town. But a dedicated Downtown Development group, in conjunction with preservationists and Main Street, saw to it that these outlying businesses did not strip the soul from the downtown commercial section, which today is full of life, its historic structures housing successful retail businesses plus many restaurants and bars, its plentiful parking areas full of cars, and its sidewalks busy with window shoppers.

From the Anglicized version of an early settler's name (Peter av Hammerdal) came the town's name. In the 1830s Hammerdal, a Swedish seafarer who had purchased land in the area to start a timber plantation, began shipping masts, tar, pitch, and other products for the New Orleans maritime industry from the head of navigation on the

Natalbany River. The spot where the tracks of the New Orleans, Jackson & Great Northern Railroad crossed his trail in 1854 was first called Hammond's Crossing.

The coming of the railroad brought new settlers and land speculation, soon turning Hammond into a center of commerce and transportation. During the early years of the Civil War it was the location of a Confederate shoe factory operated by Charles Emery Cate, who purchased three hundred acres of prime land for a tannery and sawmill as well as a home and factory. When Federal troops destroyed the shoe factory in 1862, Cate laid out the city in orderly grids stretching from the rail line, lining the streets with live oaks, many of which continue to provide lush shady landscapes in the historic neighborhoods. Cate operated a hotel, sold building lots to train passengers, and also donated land for Grace Memorial Episcopal Church, which held its first service in 1876; the church was dedicated in 1888 in memory of his wife, Mertie Cate. His garden has been preserved as a downtown greenspace called Cate Square; under the spreading Hammond Oak lie Peter Hammond and his family, buried alongside "a favorite slave boy."

Surrounded by lush pine forests watered by natural springs, Hammond became a busy shipping center for the prosperous timber industry, as well as a summertime refuge for New Orleans residents fleeing yellow fever epidemics that spread with such devastating effect in the crowded urban setting. In the 1890s, a new and hardy variety of strawberry was perfected. The felicitous climate and fertile fields around Hammond proved perfectly

**Grace Memorial
Episcopal Church**

suited for this crop, and local farmers could easily ship their harvest to northern markets aboard the Crimson Flyers, bringing new prosperity as the area became known as the Strawberry Capital of America.

Hammond's downtown commercial district, centered by the intersection of Thomas Street and the railroad tracks, blossomed in this period of prosperity as well, its vulnerable wooden structures replaced with lovely embellished brick buildings after a devastating 1894 fire. The city's Historic District Commission carefully preserves the character, overseeing restorations and renovations. In 1978 the city council established the Hammond Historic District, and in 1980 much of downtown Hammond became a National Register Historic District, including seventeen blocks and about one hundred structures dating from the 1880s to the mid-1900s. In 1984 Hammond became a state Main Street community, and later in the 1980s the state legislature approved a Downtown Development District, with tax millage dedicated to upgrading and improving downtown Hammond.

The historic commercial buildings exhibit various architectural styles, from Queen Anne Revival to Art Deco and Renaissance Revival. Many of the multi-storied structures offer upstairs loft living spaces that ensure a twenty-four-hour presence downtown. When the citizens of Hammond joined together to provide input for their comprehensive future development plan, the completed study noted something remarkable about suggestions for the historic downtown area: "how little is actually proposed to change. What is best about the plan is perhaps

Downtown Hammond

all that it *doesn't* do: it doesn't propose the road closures, superblocks, privatization of public space, and concessions to the automobile that have been shown to degrade the quality of places. It proposes a program for preservation and enhancement."

In fact, the Hammond Comprehensive Master Plan adopted in June 2011 recognized and applauded the ongoing efforts of concerned citizens and city administrations to keep the downtown area economically viable while preserving its historic character. "The city," said the plan, "has worked to revitalize the Downtown and its adjacent historic neighborhoods. Efforts include awarding façade restoration grants, creating design review boards, and creating the Hammond Downtown Development District Authority which assesses a tax millage solely for use within the District. The Downtown is already an exemplary mixed-use, compact, walkable neighborhood."

Which is not to say that it has always been easy. The director of the Downtown Development District, who also serves as the Main Street manager, notes that when the historic structures were built in Hammond (and in just about every other little community, as well), "no one expected future generations to walk off and move out to the suburbs thinking that shopping and doing business on a two thousand-foot slab of concrete would replace the sidewalks downtown or the architecture of the buildings that in some cases even had materials imported from other countries. We left the American pride . . . for awhile, and sadly, when we town people woke up and remembered our heritage and came back downtown, some of the buildings

were deteriorating, if not gone forever. Thank goodness," the director continues, "there are hundreds and thousands of hardy people who did come back and are rebuilding the dream we broke and are making amends by fixing the façade, sanding the old wooden floors, shining the beauty right back into these treasures. Some of us even live downtown—who knew convenience living could be so beautiful! We're lucky to have building owners who have done the right thing most of the time when renovating the historic buildings and who respect the Main Streets of Hammond."

Flanking the commercial district are shady residential neighborhoods filled with fine historic homes, the campus of Southeastern Louisiana University—which is the third largest institution of higher learning in the state—and the

Train depot

depot where passengers can still hop on Amtrak trains. Among the downtown commercial district's anchors are the grand Columbia Theatre, opened in 1928 and today, after a multi-million dollar renovation, a major cultural venue on the North Shore, and just across the street, the Tangipahoa Parish Library–Hammond Branch, which has been the recipient of DDD and Main Street façade grants. The Columbia, with its incredible acoustics, hosts musical and theatrical productions, and even has a couple of Pajamas and Play performances, kid-friendly plays with the audience in PJs enjoying milk and cookies. The Ritz Theater, built in 1905, is another important structure that was recently renovated with grant funds and private investment monies. Following historic guidelines for preservation, the Ritz has been divided into apartments on the inside while preserving the vintage visual impact outside, and today it is called the jewel of Cypress Street, a magnet for future rehab investments. Says the Main Street/DDD director, "When new businesses consider coming to Hammond, they are interested in what the buildings look like, whether they are preserved and cared for. They want pride and prosperity showing on the streets."

Another downtown success story involves two structures on bustling East Thomas Street marked by huge neon signage, one saying CAFÉ that had housed a popular eatery, the other saying ROSENBLUMS which was the name of the fine old store in that structure. These properties had been allowed to deteriorate until a new owner began the reclamation process—just as the disastrous Hurricane Katrina rendered labor and

appropriate materials immensely hard to get. For the first time, the DDD of Hammond and the state Division of Historic Preservation helped the owner meet these unique challenges by giving time extensions regarding completion dates for grant eligibility. Now these significant structures have been beautifully renovated to house business tenants on the street level with residential condos above, prime examples of the working partnerships at every level of private and governmental involvement that sometimes

move mountains to support the revitalization of Louisiana's historic downtowns.

The Main Street Community District in Hammond covers the same area as the Downtown Development District and includes the slightly smaller National Register Historic District, all working toward the same goal. As the Hammond Comprehensive Master Plan clearly spells out, that goal is to "protect the buildings and landscapes the people often value most about the city. Preservation and renewal of historic buildings, districts, and landscapes affirm the continuity and evolution of society. All places change over time and adaptive re-use and strategic new construction is encouraged in the Historic District, yet block dimensions, street types, building types, and specific buildings would be protected and restored where possible."

Hammond shows off its lively downtown area with signature events like Art In April, Second Saturday Sidewalk Sales, the big block party called Take It To The Tracks, Strawberry Jam 'N Toast to the Arts, Hot August Night, and Starry November Night, each encouraging traffic to the downtown streets and businesses for art exhibits, drama and dance performances, live music, good food, spectacular shopping, and seasonal celebrations. Since downtown Hammond was designated a certified Louisiana Cultural District in 2009, art sales are tax free.

These inviting special events are designed to increase traffic and appreciation of Hammond's historic downtown area, and they do that magnificently. But really, the residents simply love their downtown *every* day! It is the repository of the community's character and collective heritage, and, as the comprehensive planners found, the prime example of what is best about Hammond and what is best about the people who are courageous enough to invest their energies and funds into keeping it that way. It's not just about a sense of place, although that is certainly strong here in Hammond—these old brick walls ooze history. It's also about the people, from the early settlers with the vision to build such fine structures to the contemporary patrons, occupants, and investors who struggle to preserve them and breathe new life into them so that succeeding generations may enjoy them.

Houma

Population: 33,727

Terrebonne means "good earth" in French, and the rich alluvial soil meant that sugar was king in the Houma area for most of the nineteenth century. At one time there were close to one hundred sugar mills operating in the parish, with as many as five hundred growers producing more than one hundred million pounds of sugar in peak years, hauling the crop to the mills via mule-drawn wagons first and later dummy trains or barges along the bayous. Each plantation had its elegant home. Some of these fine homes still stand—Ardoyne, Southdown, Magnolia, and Ellendale—while others like Belle Grove are gone, their locations marked only by the ancient live oaks that once enfolded them, a shaded spot in the vast expanses of open cane fields. The last mill operating in Terrebonne Parish was at Southdown Plantation, where the raw sugar mill and refinery built by the Minor family had been producing since the early 1830s and where the state sugar industry was saved when a new variety of hardy imported cane was shared with growers whose crops had been devastated by mosaic disease. When the Southdown mill shut down at the end of grinding season in

1978, it was dismantled and sent to Guatemala. Many Houma area farmers still plant cane, though it is hauled now to mills outside the parish.

In 1822 the state legislature carved Terrebonne Parish out of Lafourche Interior Parish. Because of the area's large population of Acadian-descended French speakers, when the local newspaper, the *Houma Courier*, began operation in 1878, half of its pages were printed in French and half in English. Houma Indians, driven south to this area from the convergence of the Red and Mississippi rivers, had settled the place even earlier. When the town of Houma was founded in the 1830s along the banks of Bayou Terrebonne on lands donated by Hubert M. Belanger and his son-in-law Richard H. Grinage, it took the name of the Houma, but it was also called the Venice of North America, located as it was at the confluence of six bayous that had all once been tributaries of the Mississippi. In the early days, Terrebonne's prolific waterways provided both livelihood and transportation; roads eventually developed alongside these bayous that horse-drawn wagons and later automobiles traveled.

The region certainly had been blessed with abundant natural resources, its waters teeming with oysters and fish, its forests thick with ancient cypress. Around the turn of the century, Houma was one of the country's largest producers of oysters; some 175 million oysters were shipped in 1905 (expert shuckers could open as many as seven thousand oysters a day), and instead of gravel, oyster or clam shells paved many parish roads. The shrimp drying process introduced in 1873 by Cantonese Lee Yim combined with

Blum and Bergeron, Inc. employees

the advent of the shrimp trawl to make shrimping another vital economic force. Blum and Bergeron, Inc., a shrimp packing company, has been in business since 1910 and in their Main Street facility since 1921. The expansive stands of giant old-growth tidewater cypress trees, some towering up to 150 feet tall, especially in the Gibson and Chacahoula swamps, gave rise to a booming lumber trade in an area, where in the late nineteenth century, timberland sold for as little as a dollar or two an acre; lumber, shingles, even railroad crossties were produced as if the resources would last forever. Enough Terrebonne residents were involved in the nineteenth-century fur industry that at least one local church held Christmas services in the spring after the trappers and hunters brought their families back to town from the marshes where they spent the winters.

Incorporated in 1843, Houma became the seat of government as well as the location of the many small businesses required to support the outlying unincorporated areas. It became the center of religious life as well, once the Catholic parish of St. Francis de Sales was established in 1847 (its magnificent Gothic cathedral remains a riveting focus of downtown Houma today). "Exceptionally well located, geographically, to command the trade of the rich parish of Terrebonne," was the description of the town in 1906 when the *Houma Courier* published a snazzy magazine edition entitled *Terrebonne Parish—Her Undeveloped Resources and Manufacturing Interests: The Capitalists' Chance for Investment.*

While growth ebbed and flowed with the vagaries of the sugar industry—always at the mercy of fluctuations

St. Francis de Sales Church

of weather and market price, crop diseases, and post-bellum labor challenges—Houma saw a big jump in its population and prosperity around the turn of the century, with new industries established to turn it into "a living town breathing for the first time the breath of commercial life." The paper proudly listed some of the early twentieth-century industrial developments—two banks, two cotton gins, a moss gin, a barrel factory, a cistern factory, several mercantile establishments, and a number of stores and businesses.

"All things considered, Houma offers splendid inducements for the capitalist and home-seeker," promised the newspaper. "Life here can be made pleasant as well as profitable. Social conditions are all that could be desired. Our people are a quiet, law-abiding and God-fearing class. Our climate is mild, the health of the town excellent and most of the conveniences and necessities that modern life demands can be obtained in Houma. Where on earth can the home-seeker find a better place than this?" The local judge, commenting on the state of law and order, waxed eloquent, finding Houma's population "probably the most even tempered, good natured, law abiding people in all Louisiana, by nature of an amiable disposition; the descendants of the original Acadian settlers appear to have found in the caressing salt breezes and normally delightful climate of our gulf shore and bayou inlets just the climactic influence to enrich and beautify an already lovable character."

The special edition bragged that the town population had increased from 429 in 1860 to over five thousand in

1906, that Houma banks had over half a million dollars in deposits, the town had "telegraphic communication with the rest of the world through the Western Union," and boasted a high rate of telephone users, 331 subscribers, and as anyone knows, "extensive patronage of the telephone indicates progress and prosperity in a community."

The 1906 edition also noted that, "There are many who believe and predict that Terrebonne will be an important oil field some day." It would not be long before it was determined that Terrebonne Parish did indeed sit upon some extensive and valuable deposits. The first successful local oil well, a land-based well only 2,998 feet deep, was drilled in Houma in 1918, just a couple of years after the area's first gas wells. With the birth of the energy industry and subsequent developments in support services, Houma

was booming. WPA works projects in the 1930s, as the town celebrated its centennial, provided funding to overlay downtown's shell roads with pavement, and by 1940 the population had topped ten thousand.

As oil production in the area increased, an airport became a necessity, and one was constructed from former sugarcane fields by 1939, initially comprised of grass landing areas accessed by a clamshell strip. During World War II, the Houma Naval Air Station was home to a squadron of blimps assigned to protect merchant shipping from German submarines in the Gulf of Mexico. No ship escorted by the blimps was ever attacked, but the airships provided plenty of local excitement, especially when a couple escaped their moorings in windstorms and their depth charges blew to smithereens one startled farmer's potato patch.

When the Intracoastal Canal was dug through town in the 1930s, a drawbridge connected east and west Houma, its spans having to be raised to permit boat passage. This proved quite an irritant to local residents once traffic on the waterway became heavy, especially during wartime with much of the shipping diverted from dangerous Gulf waters to this important inland route. Contemporary accounts of the times cite a number of expectant mothers from the east side who were delayed in reaching the hospital on the west side, their babies subsequently delivered in vehicles waiting for the bridge to close.

Cultural tourism has been a boon to Terrebonne Parish, especially after being featured in such films as *Crazy in Alabama*, *A Lesson Before Dying*, and the IMAX feature *Hurricane on the Bayou.* Besides great Cajun food, music, and dancing, the Houma area offers visitors the opportunity to experience its cultural heritage first-hand by traversing the cypress swamps with such illustrious native-born tour guides as the son of the late beloved professional snake-catcher Annie Miller and the nationally known "Cajun Man" singer Black Guidry. The sugarcane industry is memorialized at Southdown Plantation, the historic home and surrounding 4.46 acres now owned by the Terrebonne Historical and Cultural Society. Southdown is open year-round for tours and special events like its immensely popular arts and crafts marketplaces. On Barrow Street, the Regional Military Museum honors veterans from all branches of the military who served in United States wars.

But by the end of the twentieth century, the downtown Houma area straddling Bayou Terrebonne, like many a downtown district across the country, was in a state of decline, suburbs and strip malls having drained its vitality and drawn away its patrons. Fires had taken their toll, especially in the late nineteenth century, leaving a triangular building near the courthouse forever known as Smoky Row because the two-story wooden structure there smoked but did not burn down. A devastating 1970 gas line explosion demolished other downtown structures, killed a fire chief and a couple of workmen, and singed the trees on the courthouse square. The landmark 1860 courthouse, a beloved four-faced clock in its tower and the gallows for carrying out death sentences on its third floor, was torn down in 1937 to make way for a more modern structure.

Smoky Row

This newer parish courthouse and its pleasant park, shaded by oaks planted in 1886, remained busy. So did the multitude of historic homes turned into offices for local attorneys, despite the populace's reputation as "quiet, law-abiding and God-fearing citizens." Yet it became obvious that something had to be done to halt the decline of historic downtown Houma. The Houma Downtown Development Corporation was formed and combined forces with the Main Street program implemented in 1985 to breathe new life into the area, developing inviting bayouside walkways, a children's park and marina docking facilities, a folklife cultural center, and the wonderful Bayou Terrebonne Waterlife Museum.

Façade grants and tax incentives have encouraged the rehabbing of commercial structures, and a beautiful

Bayou Walk officially opened in April 2011. The walk, intended to help build community and foster a pleasant pedestrian environment downtown according to *The Daily Comet*, provides a place for visitors to enjoy bayou views and for locals to stroll, exercise, and take time to visit with one another. The Houma Area Convention and Visitors Bureau has compiled a walking tour of forty-four historic sites. Special events designed to draw participants to the downtown area, planned in conjunction with the Downtown Business Association and the Terrebonne Parish Consolidated Government, include live concerts in the courthouse square from March through October, a spring evening art stroll with local art exhibits placed in various buildings throughout the historic district, a special exposition of wildlife artists and carvers, month-long activities in November as part of Louisiana Main to Main, and a Christmas parade down Main Street (Houma goes in for Mardi Gras in a big way, too). The Houma-Thibodaux area was recently honored by *Site Selection* magazine as a national leader in business investment in 2010.

The seven thousand-square-foot Bayou Terrebonne Waterlife Museum, next to the bayou on the site of early oyster packing and shrimp canning facilities, has interactive exhibits that celebrate traditional mainstays of the Houma area economy, from early fur-trapping and fisheries to sugarcane farming, logging, and the oil and gas industry. The gigantic alligator is beyond belief, and the Wetlands Wall is a forty-six-foot curving mural following the eco-line from the Gulf of Mexico and barrier islands through saltwater marshes, estuaries, freshwater lakes, and the parish's "high land," eight or nine feet above sea level. This is, after all, the Heart of America's Wetland.

The Waterlife Museum and its bayouside park may be rented for special events, meetings, and weddings, as can the Terrebonne Folklife Culture Center, located in a former gentlemen's club occupied in later years by a legendary game warden famous for shootouts and a talented dog that howled "Home on the Range." Dedicated to the preservation of Cajun heritage and folklore, the Folklife Center has cultural exhibits of Cajun woodworking tools, duck decoys, and Native American artifacts, and it offers classes and workshops teaching everything from conversational French to Cajun dance and Indian crafts.

**Above: Terrebonne Folklife Culture Center
Opposite page: Bayou Terrebonne Waterlife Museum**

The former city hall on Main Street is now the setting for dramatic productions, and other downtown structures are finding new life in new incarnations. One longtime focal point of historic downtown Houma was St. Matthew's Episcopal Church, chartered in 1855 by Louisiana's Fighting Bishop, Leonidas Polk. When the *Courier* published a commemorative issue marking the 175th anniversary of the founding of Terrebonne Parish, it remarked that St. Matthew's had withstood the ravages of fire, hurricanes, and war. Alas, the cypress structure, erected in 1892 to replace an earlier one built on property donated by charter member Robert Ruffin Barrow, burned to the ground in 2011.

Its determined congregation vows it shall rise again, and so it shall. Such are the trials of Main Street communities, and the resilience.

Le Petit Theatre in the old city hall

St. Matthew's Episcopal Church prior to 2011 fire

Leesville

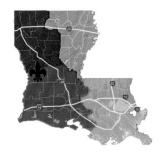

Population: 6,612

Leesville was named for a respected Southern general and is the seat of government of a parish possibly named for the first American president's home. However, for some years after the Louisiana Purchase, the Leesville area wasn't part of the United States at all. Instead, it fell in the lawless territory known as No Man's Land, crossed only with trepidation and armed escort. The narrow strip between the Sabine and Calcasieu rivers was the object of ongoing border disputes, first between France and Spain, and then after 1803 between the United States and Spain, with both parties claiming the territory and neither enforcing law and order.

The establishment of Fort Jesup to the north brought a stabilizing military presence to this lawless neutral strip in 1822. Today Leesville is the home of the country's fifth largest military installation, Fort Polk, but the city began as a sleepy lumber town that wasn't incorporated until 1900. When it was established along the banks of Castor Bayou in 1871, it was named for Gen. Robert E. Lee by the city founder Dr. Edmund E. Smart's father,

R. Smart. Dr. Smart subdivided his plantation and named several of the streets for his wife and daughters. His 1850s home still stands on the corner of First and Lula streets, the only surviving antebellum building in Leesville's lovely downtown National Register Historic District.

A bunch of gentlemen, so the story goes, were lounging around on the porch of Dr. Smart's store one day discussing the affairs of the world when the topic of the naming of the parish arose. Who should happen by but Uncle Balaam Jones, a former slave, with his fine mule. "What's the name of your mule, Uncle Balaam?" the gathering inquired. "Why, I named him after Mr. Joe Moore's horse Vernon, the fastest horse in the parish, because he's the fastest mule in the parish!" So maybe

Vernon Parish was not named for George Washington's Mount Vernon after all, or maybe it was, but the fastest mule makes a better tale.

Driving the early economy in this verdant piney woods area was the timber industry, which boomed once the arrival of the Kansas City Southern Railway in 1897 allowed increased marketing and shipping capabilities, bringing a taste of prosperity to the area. By 1920 there were eleven operating sawmills in the parish, including some of the largest in the world. As early as 1905, the principal mills at Leesville were the Gulf Land and Lumber Company and Nona Mills Company of Louisiana, each cutting 100,000 feet daily and employing more than three hundred mill hands and loggers.

Gulf Land and Lumber actually had three mills, plus offices, a hotel and tenant houses, a depot and post office, a market, a schoolhouse, and a doctor's office, with several locomotives bringing in four trainloads of forty-eight cars full of logs to the mill pond daily. At Nona Mills there were machine and blacksmith shops, mill offices, a physician's office, a barbershop, a hotel and boarding house, an ice house, and a commissary. Nona Mills operated Leesville's largest store with grocery, dry goods, and hardware departments and was a large contributor to Leesville's economy. Called the leading industry of Leesville in a 1907 newspaper report, Nona Mills was conscientious about contributing to community improvements, making possible the town waterworks, ice plant and hotel, as well as the local baseball team, militia company, and brass band. In 1908 Nona Mills funded a new and sorely

Vernon Bank

One downtown bank, built in 1904, survived the 1907 fire. Other outstanding structures downtown were built after the fire, including the Lyons Building, constructed by a wealthy lumberman in the Italianate style, with arched windows and imposing cornices; this was the longtime home of the Happy Hour Café and the local dentist. The thirty-five-room Leesville Hotel was constructed in 1907 and counted among its guests the infamous Bonnie and Clyde, as well as colorful Louisiana governor Huey Long, who was asked to leave by owner Dr. Daniel Willis for using language offensive to the ladies present. After Dr. Willis was killed in an automobile accident, his widow had his body laid out for viewing in the hotel dining room, which proved so unappetizing to prospective diners that it subsequently closed.

needed concrete fire station for the town, complete with two firemen and horses, a large chemical engine, a hook and ladder wagon, and a hose wagon.

The downtown commercial district along the railroad tracks quickly filled with substantial structures supplying the needs of the lumber industry, all made, quite naturally, of wood—mostly pine, highly *flammable* pine. That's why today most of Leesville's historic structures date from 1907. A disastrous fire that year began in a hotel and quickly destroyed most of the wooden buildings in the business district. Replacement structures were wisely made of brick, and today the historic downtown district is a lively and appealing area, its vintage structures housing new businesses, venues for special events, and even some upstairs spaces for loft living that will ensure around-the-clock vitality.

Lyons Building

Downtown Leesville

Slightly later structures include the 1915 Dreamland Theater which is now a special event setting called Celebrations; the 1928 Merchants and Farmers Bank in the English Revival style; and the Post Office, built by the WPA during the Depression in Art Deco style with an interior sculpture created by Duncan Ferguson, a New York artist brought to Louisiana to start LSU's art school. Overnight accommodations are provided in the Historic District in the Booker-Lewis House, built for the Nona Mills bookkeeper around the turn of the century in Queen Anne-Colonial Revival style, with fanciful yellow pine trim work.

Presiding regally over this commercial district is the dome-crowned Vernon Parish Courthouse, an enormous Beaux Arts structure with impressive Corinthian columns. It is the third courthouse on the site since Leesville was made the parish seat upon the creation of Vernon Parish in 1871.

The Leesville Historic District Commission enforces the upholding of the strict standards of the National Register of Historic Places and encourages preservation downtown with the guiding motto "Pride in our heritage, pride in our future," a welcome change from previous administrations that demolished hundreds of vintage structures. The recently established Main Street program provides assistance through its access to rehabilitation grant funds, in cooperation with the very active parish tourist commission, also housed in the courthouse.

Opposite page: Vernon Parish Courthouse

The Vernon Arts Council presents a series of cultural events and concerts and for decades has sponsored Mayfest, an annual arts and crafts festival in the Leesville Downtown Historic District offering fun, food, and entertainment along with the arts. Also in the heart of the historic district is Gallery One Ellleven (yes, there are three *l*'s), an artists' co-op gallery with changing exhibits and events, and another welcome addition to the cultural scene called ArtWalk in spring and fall downtown. During growing season, the downtown Third Street Market has fresh produce and more, and there are Mardi Gras and Christmas parades and festivities, plus an annual Holiday Tour of Homes sponsored by the Tour of Homes Association. All these activities draw residents and visitors to Leesville's historic district and encourage an appreciation of local history and heritage while supporting the homegrown business and arts communities.

The restored railroad depot offers the best opportunity to gain an appreciation of Leesville's unique history, especially as it involved the railroad. The Kansas City Southern Railroad reached Leesville in 1897, and a roundhouse was built to repair and switch steam locomotives. The first diesel passenger train arrived in 1938 (the last one departed in 1968). The 1916 depot, listed on the National Register of Historic Places, now houses the free Museum of West Louisiana; also on site are a dogtrot house, a shotgun house, and a section house, all examples of local architectural styles around the turn of the century. Archaeological artifacts and fossils, logging and farm implements, railroad memorabilia, and vintage household furnishings are on display, along with a fascinating collection of pine knots and a cross-section of the trunk of the 1982 state champion longleaf pine. But the most interesting exhibits here are scale models made by the talented and obviously very patient Mr. Elbert Dyess. These models, created in pine in painstaking detail, include a working sawmill complete with waterwheel and a detailed replica of his grandparents' homestead where they raised twenty-two children, the simple farmhouse surrounded by barns, sugar mill, livestock, and even a moonshine still. In December the museum hosts its Elegant Affair open house.

Even more important than the railroad in the later

Museum of West Louisiana

development of the area has been the military presence. In 1941 the U.S. Army established Camp Polk in Leesville just after the Louisiana Maneuvers brought nearly half a million soldiers to utilize more than three thousand square miles in Central Louisiana, where they practiced modern tactics and tested new equipment in preparation for World War II. Once the camp opened, Leesville's population jumped from 3,500 to 18,000. So many saloons catered to off-duty servicemen along Lower Third Street—the Silver Slipper, the Siamese, the Cave Bar, the Red Diamond, and the Red Hound that was a favorite hangout of George F. Patton and Omar Bradley on Upper Third—that the unwritten social rule was that "nice girls" would not be caught dead south of Harriet Street, since Fort Polk had a shuttle bus station there with droves of soldiers hanging

around. Today Fort Polk, named for Episcopal Bishop and Confederate Gen. Leonidas Polk, is the fifth largest military installation in the nation, covering more than 200,000 acres.

Fort Polk is the home of the elite national Joint Readiness Training Center for the Department of Defense, preparing personnel for overseas warfare with accurately recreated terrains and townscapes, where soldiers from the international community as well as American troops prepare to face all types of situations in the global war against terrorism. On base is a military museum, open to the public and full of exhibits from the Revolutionary War to the present. Fort Polk is also one of the state's largest employers, with more than $1.5 billion economic impact, and it is certainly the dominant force in

Leesville's present-day economy, with more than 22,000 active military personnel, as well as their families and many retirees who opt to stay in the area.

And it is no wonder so many servicemen choose to remain in the region after retirement. The nearby Kisatchie National Forest has pine forests, rolling hills, and clear streams for hiking, fishing, swimming, canoeing, camping, hunting, horseback riding, picnicking, birding, and other recreational pursuits. The surrounding region boasts a number of wildlife management areas and some large lakes—five thousand-acre Vernon Lake, two thousand-acre Anacoco Lake, and Toledo Bend Reservoir, with 1,200 miles of shoreline and world-famous bass fishing. Scenic drives pass outlying historic sites like the 1864 Civil War breastworks at Burr Ferry on the Sabine River, unique grave houses in several local cemeteries, Holly Grove Methodist Church established in the 1830s, and the sites of several socialistic experimental colonies. Notable among the latter was the New Llano Cooperative Colony that occupied 20,000 acres a few miles south of Leesville, with productive farming and manufacturing operations, a school, infirmary, hotel, and recreational facilities. This was an offshoot of the Llano del Rio Cooperative Colony begun in 1915 near the San Gabriel Mountains of California and abandoned in 1918 when sixty families moved to Louisiana's Vernon Parish to establish New Llano. Until the 1930s, the community functioned as a corporate-run socialist Utopian society, with its citizens pooling and sharing resources and wealth.

Today in the Leesville area, all it takes is comparing the proliferation of Tex-Mex restaurants with the few Cajun/seafood restaurants and it becomes obvious: This ain't Cajun Country, Toteaux, or Kansas either. This is west central Louisiana, which has its own unique historical influences and a very different heritage. With its close proximity to Texas and the surrounding piney woods, Leesville provides a wonderful contrast to its francophone neighbors to the south.

Minden

Population: 13,082

Fasching is the colorful German pre-Lenten carnival celebration, a season officially beginning in the eleventh month on the eleventh day at the eleventh hour. So what's with the celebration of *Fasching* in a state famed for Mardi Gras madness, and why are there so many Nutcrackers in the Christmas decorations? Welcome to Minden, the northwest Louisiana city known for its beautiful brick-paved downtown streets and for its German heritage in a state most often considered French.

It was in the early 1830s that a group of German Utopians, led by the mysterious Countess von Leon, settled just outside Minden. The countess was the widow of Count von Leon, otherwise known as Bernhard Muller, a German mystic who led a group of followers in an attempt to build an earthly utopia while awaiting the second coming of Christ; the count died of yellow fever along the way, but his widow and followers settled near Minden at the exact latitude of Jerusalem. One of three such socialist religious colonies founded in the United States in the early nineteenth century and now commemorated through the

Germantown Colony Museum, this settlement successfully operated on a communal basis, while farming cotton, for four decades.

Minden itself was established by Charles Hans Veeder, a New Yorker who named it for his ancestral home in Germany. In 1836 he built a hilltop hostel called the Rock Inn near Bayou Dorcheat and soon thereafter laid out a town shaped like a parallelogram. The bayou, now a Louisiana Scenic Stream, was the center of early economic life, with several boat landings and warehouses and commercial establishments eventually extending more than a mile along the east bank, allowing Minden to serve as an all-important shipping point for goods from all over North Louisiana.

By 1838 the town had received one of the first state charters for a public school, Minden Academy (the high school of today sits on that very same site). In 1850 this would become the Minden Female Academy, where young ladies from across the south came to receive a first-rate education from highly qualified instructors whose presence greatly enhanced the cultural atmosphere of Minden. In 1854 the academy was upgraded to the status of a college.

This growing community came to be recognized as a center for culture and education along an otherwise rough-and-tumble frontier. Church congregations came together in worship, Methodists in 1839, Baptists in 1844, and Episcopalians in the early 1850s. In 1849 Veeder succumbed to the lure of the California Gold Rush, but Minden attracted large numbers of other settlers coming

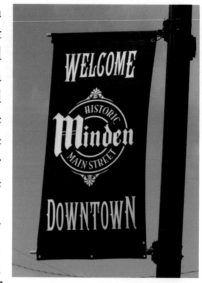

from England, South Carolina, and Georgia. It was formally incorporated as a town by the Louisiana Legislature of 1850, and all those church folks must have had a hand in laying out the rules for acceptable behavior included as ordinances in the city charter.

According to research by local historian John Agan, the original town charter, in effect for the latter half of the nineteenth century with some of its ordinances still enforced when Minden was recognized as a city in 1926, included regulations against quarreling or being drunk at church; spitting on floors in public buildings or on sidewalks; riding a horse into a home or business; rapidly driving horses or mules through town; camping with a fire downtown; throwing shot or rocks with elastic slingshots; and attaching tin boxes to the tail of a horse, mule, cow, hog, or dog to frighten or annoy the unfortunate animal. Other ordinances aimed to deter vagrants, defined as those "wandering the streets with no visible means of support, habitual drunkards, female street walkers, and all persons able to work who have not work or occupation and who live on the wages of their minor children or wives." Public drunkenness, "any person being drunk or intoxicated for 2 or 3 days within the limits of the town of Minden," was punishable by being jailed and "kept from drinking strong drink, until sober." As late as 1926 the downtown speed limit for trucks was all of 10 mph, automobiles 15 mph.

During the Civil War, as many as fifteen thousand Confederate troops were quartered in camps just east of Minden throughout the winter of 1864-65, and when the city surrendered in late May 1865 it was occupied by members of the 61ˢᵗ U.S. Colored Troops. The Reconstruction era proved so trying that at one point local voters wrote in the name of a well-known local bull rather than vote for a Carpetbagger candidate.

In 1871 Minden was chosen as parish seat of the newly created Webster Parish. Within the next decade the railroad finally reached town, giving the local economy a long-lasting boost. The Louisiana and Arkansas Railroad had its headquarters in Minden, and railroad owners opened the Minden Lumber Mill, which was among the world's largest. During the Great Blizzard of February 1890, Minden recorded the coldest temperature ever in the state, minus sixteen degrees.

To Minden as to most other small towns, the Great Depression brought heartache and struggle. The economic calamity was accentuated by other disasters. In February 1933 nearly a fourth of downtown Minden was destroyed in a devastating fire; the volunteer fire chief died as a result of a heart attack suffered battling the blaze. In April Minden's largest bank, one of only two in town, failed. In May a powerful tornado killed twenty-eight residents and caused more than $1 million in damages, destroying 20 percent of Minden's residences. A summer flood ruined a

third of the crops in the area. But the tenacious little town survived. In fact it grew and thrived, especially once a large ammunition plant began operation there.

Now with a diversified economy, Minden remains a city that "treasures its past and respects its roots." Minden's Historic Residential District encompasses an outstanding collection of vintage structures, more than seventy total, all residences except for two churches, the 1923 Gothic Revival Presbyterian Church with its Germanic half-timbering and St. John's Episcopal Church, built in 1950 but in the historic Gothic style so beloved by Episcopalians. Just north of downtown and well shaded by mature trees, the district includes architectural styles ranging from

Downtown Minden

Above: Holland Crawford Insurance located in the former Bank of Minden
Opposite page: Citizens Bank and Trust and surrounding buildings

1850s Greek Revival to Victorian, and from Queen Anne Revival through the Spanish Colonial. The area is easily considered the most outstanding collection of historic homes in Webster Parish. The largest concentration may be seen on Broadway, called "the city's grand residential rue," with larger lots and well-preserved, multi-storied houses set back from the street. The district is protected and preserved by the Minden Historic Residential District Association.

It is the Historic Downtown Business District that remains the hub of city and parish government as well as the center of the medical and banking communities. The district is very much alive today and filled with hustle and bustle as shoppers patronize specialty stores, antiques and gift shops, photography studios, jewelers, barbers, and fine eateries. Main Street is still paved with rosy bricks laid in 1917, and it is lined with delightful historic commercial structures, many made of brick after the lessons taught by the Depression-era downtown fire. The impressive Citizens Bank and Trust Company building, individually listed on the National Register of Historic Places, was built in 1910 and beautifully renovated in 2001, a bas-relief eagle centered in its classical parapet and the entrance flanked by freestanding columns. A shady park with a gazebo welcomes strollers to pause awhile and contemplate the charm of Minden's downtown, which in recent years has become a favored setting for Hollywood filmmakers.

The Historic Residential District, Downtown Historical Business District, and a section of Old East Union Hwy. 80 are all included in an Art and Cultural District permitting

Above and opposite page: Downtown Minden

sales tax exemptions on original art purchased there and also allowing both commercial and residential structures to receive historic preservation and rehab tax credits. In the heart of downtown Minden, City Art Works—called the hub of cultural recreation—includes an art gallery and artists' studios, plus space for lessons in everything from stained glass making to line dancing, jewelry creation, floral design, and drawing. The Cultural Crossroads arts organization oversees arts programming at "The Farm" on East Union in the cultural district, including Arts in Education, The Farm Project, Spring Arts Festival, Art on Broadway, and Pearl Music Fest. Downtown also features the Dorcheat Historical Museum with a media center, a gift shop, murals, dioramas, a log cabin, and all

sorts of fascinating artifacts. The unique "Art in the Alley" showcases enlarged reproductions of original art works.

Minden joined the state Main Street program in 1987 and has enthusiastically embraced its mission to preserve history by promoting economic revitalization and rehabilitation of historic buildings. An active Main Street program, assisted by Louisiana Main Street, has enabled downtown Minden to reap the benefits of thousands of dollars in façade and revitalization grants. The Main Street board and its veteran manager, who is also the director of economic and downtown development, strive to strengthen public participation and make downtown a fun and profitable place by sponsoring a number of special events and festivals designed to draw appreciative visitors to the area. Main to Main Trade Days, for example, features fifty miles of food, fun, and shopping from Minden all the way to Arkansas.

But it's during Christmas season that Minden really shines, and beginning in 2011 the town joined the long-established but recently reconfigured Holiday Tour of Lights, FaLaLaLouisiana, connecting Shreveport, Minden, West Monroe, Monroe, Natchitoches, Alexandria, and Pineville (no Texas connections any more), and featuring miles of holiday lights and seasonal events beginning around Thanksgiving. In Minden, the celebration begins even earlier with the Fasching Fifth Season Festival, starting November 11 and paying tribute to the town's proud German heritage with parades, thousands of lights, historic tours, and live music. This German equivalent of Mardi Gras, according to the Main Street manager,

educates visitors about the city's "German heritage, food, and entertainment; the season ends Ash Wednesday. It's a different part of the Louisiana culture aside from the French culture. It will be a different taste of Louisiana." Main Street Minden for a number of years sponsored a Mardi Gras parade, but this Fasching Festival is even more appropriate.

Minden's Christmas season also includes a cemetery ghost walk through the Old Minden Cemetery, a Deck the Gallery art show, a Holiday Open House sponsored by specialty shops, Wrap It Up Downtown with shopping specials and visits from Santa, the Lions Club Christmas parade, and a Community Chorus Candlelight Concert. And as hundreds of erect Nutcrackers made of everything from fiberglass to wood and lights stand guard and the hills are alive with the sound of . . . *polkas* . . . , Minden celebrates the season in its own style as a way of honoring its own unique history and heritage, a lovingly preserved past that is cherished not just during the holidays but every day of the year.

Morgan City

Population: 12,404

The wonderful thing about the statewide Main Street program is that each community astutely identifies and builds upon its uniqueness. Morgan City is the perfect example.

At first glance this seems to be the quintessential lovely Main Street community, its picturesque vintage structures elbow-to-elbow along an appealing commercial row. *Discover Downtown Morgan City* say the colorful banners flying from the light standards. But look again. Here, one side of Front Street really *is* that quintessential commercial community; but along the other side of the street snakes a towering floodwall, above which may be seen docked shrimp boats and other vessels. Stairs and walkways make this floodwall a popular tourist attraction, but its main function is safety.

This is what keeps the rushing waters of the Atchafalaya River out of the streets of Morgan City, especially when spring overflow from the Mississippi is diverted along this

channel. Over the centuries the Mississippi River has changed its course to the Gulf more than a few times and has for years been tempted to jump into the channel of the Atchafalaya, which offers a shorter route with a steeper slope. The disastrous 1927 flood sent a huge volume of Mississippi water down the 135-mile Atchafalaya channel, widening and deepening what had been a considerably smaller riverbed; in places the depth is now one hundred feet.

To keep the Mississippi on its current course, the Army Corps of Engineers has constructed immense control structures at Old River, shutting off the limited natural flow from the Mississippi into the Atchafalaya but capable, in times of severe flooding, of diverting nearly half of the Mississippi's maximum flow of three million cubic feet per second into the Atchafalaya and parallel floodways. This diversion would prevent dangerous flooding along the lower Mississippi at the major population centers of Baton Rouge and New Orleans, but could cause enormous problems for settlements along the Atchafalaya, most notably Morgan City. The Old River control structure was almost wiped out in 1973 when floodwaters undercut it, and there were record floodwaters in 2011, but it remains to be seen whether man can control the Mighty Mississippi. Old river pilot Mark Twain scoffed at efforts to confine the river, observing that man "cannot bar its path with an obstruction which it will not tear down, dance over and laugh at."

All of this leaves Morgan City, elevation seven feet, and the entire area along the lower Atchafalaya River nervously

Above: Flood levels
Opposite page: Floodwall protects and overlooks Morgan City

watching the river stages on the Mississippi each spring. The rest of the year, Morgan City can celebrate having turned adversity into advantage. The twenty-one-foot-tall concrete "Great Wall" was built in 1973 after floodwaters nearly topped the former ten-foot one; with an additional three feet of height added by boxes bolted to the top, this early wall kept the '73 floodwaters from getting into any of the buildings on Main Street, although backwater flooding was a problem in other parts of the city. Today the present wall provides tourists with the perfect vantage point to view its lovely Main Street district on one side and the bustling waterfront activity on the other.

This is, after all, the gateway to the Atchafalaya (the

name is Native American for "long river"), the largest contiguous river swamp in the United States, nearly a million acres of bottomland hardwoods, swamps, bayous, and backwater lakes as well as half a million acres of marshland, a paradise for fishermen and boaters, photographers, birders, and outdoor enthusiasts. Ecologists consider the Atchafalaya Basin one of the most productive wildlife areas in North America, and today a number of popular swamp tours introduce visitors to its wondrous wilderness area. In 1917, Atchafalaya swamplands substituted for the wilds of Africa in the first Tarzan movie Hollywood ever made.

Originally called Tigre Island and then incorporated in 1860 as Brashear City, Morgan City's strategic location made it an important staging area and military depot for the occupying Federal troops during the Civil War as they planned campaigns to capture Texas and cut off Confederate supply lines from the west. The city was renamed in 1876 for entrepreneur Charles Morgan, who had established a steamship line in the Gulf of Mexico as early as 1837, and then, as owner of the Orleans-Opelousas-and-Great-Western Railroad, made this settlement on Berwick Bay a significant transshipping point between New Orleans and Texas. Once Morgan dredged the Atchafalaya Bay Ship Channel, this sleepy little fishing village became a bustling trade center for the entire Atchafalaya basin.

Its location has continued to define Morgan City. In 1937 it became known as the jumbo shrimp capital of the world. A decade later the first producing offshore oil

First Offshore Oil Well

well out of sight of land was completed by Kerr-McGee Industries forty-three miles south of Morgan City in the Gulf of Mexico. Celebrating an economy still dependent on shrimping and black gold, Morgan City's Shrimp and Petroleum Festival is one of South Louisiana's most popular festivals and the state's oldest chartered harvest festival. Held each Labor Day weekend in Lawrence Park in the historic district, the celebration got its start in this predominantly Catholic community as a blessing of the fleet, held to ensure a bountiful harvest and a safe return as the shrimpers set out upon the perilous seas. Today it features five full days of live music, a large art exhibit at the Everett Street Art Gallery, children's activities, fireworks, a cultural and heritage expo, a culinary classic, mass in the park beneath the live oaks, a blessing of the fleet, and a water parade featuring decorated shrimp boats, pleasure boats, and even big muscle boats of the petroleum industry. It is no wonder Morgan City's Shrimp and Petroleum Festival has been named top festival by the Louisiana Association of Fairs & Festivals, a Top 20 event by the Southeast Tourism Society and the Louisiana Office of Tourism, and a Top 100 event by the American Bus Association.

The importance of the energy industry to Morgan City, birthplace of the offshore oil industry and today home of many offshore supply companies and one of the world's largest helicopter pads servicing rigs, is best understood through a visit to the fascinating International Petroleum Museum and Exposition on the banks of the Atchafalaya River at its intersection with the Intracoastal Waterway. Twice daily (except Sunday) visitors can tour

Mr. Charlie

the offshore drilling rig called "Mr. Charlie," a towering over-water training facility used by the industry, to learn about the early years of oil exploration and the functions of the drilling rigs both past and present. "Mr. Charlie," a self-contained transportable industrial island with living quarters for as many as fifty-eight workers, was the first submersible rig used in offshore production.

Besides the Shrimp and Petroleum Festival, a number of other fun and family-friendly festivals have been designed to increase traffic to the historic downtown area. Rhythms on the River spotlights live music Friday evenings in the spring, Christmas celebrations feature artists and authors and lots of seasonal shopping bargains, and gatherings like the Atchafalaya Culinary & Arts Festival celebrate the unique culture of this Cajun coast. The Eagle Expo, held

Trinity Episcopal Church

extensive park and fishing areas. The 9.5-acre Brownell Memorial Park and Carillon Tower features sixty-one bronze bells cast in Holland, weighing from 18 to 4,730 pounds.

Once Morgan City's Main Street program was established in 1997, its community combined with the nine-block historic district to encompass nineteen blocks downtown, filled with picturesque homes, churches, and commercial structures dating from the late 1800s and early 1900s. Front Street runs right along the river/floodwall and is the location of a number of boutique shops, hardware stores, and some wonderful little restaurants, like Café JoJo's, featuring fresh seafood and area specialties. Railroad Avenue is home to quite a few popular bars.

Main Street rehab incentive grants have assisted in

every February, has presentations and seminars on these majestic birds that are making a comeback in the area, and a variety of boat tours and guided nature walks highlight the spectacular natural resources and scenic swamplands around Morgan City.

The downtown area abounds in historic churches: Trinity Episcopal dating from 1877, Pharr Chapel United Methodist from 1878, and the Gothic Revival Sacred Heart Catholic Church from 1859. A unique feature of the Sacred Heart Catholic Church is a stained glass window of the expulsion of Adam and Eve from the Garden of Eden given in memory of . . . Adam and Eve Bourgeois! In the surrounding area, there are houseboat rentals and Cajun Jack's Swamp Tours, plus beautiful Lake Palourde with

704 Front Street

the revitalization of this riverfront area so that it has continued to be relevant to residents and visitors alike. One
outstanding success story has been the historic structure
at 704 Front Street, a very large, two-story vacant building on the main corridor. The building was purchased by
an enthusiastic young entrepreneur who turned the upper
floor into living quarters and opened Southern Treasures
gift shop downstairs, creating excitement and generating
business traffic that encouraged other innovative development downtown. Café JoJo's was another recipient of Main
Street incentive funding.

Morgan City is a Main Street community that
certainly capitalizes on its unique setting, its fortunes
ebbing and flowing with the river waters that have shaped
its development and its destiny. The river has been the
giver of life, watering, fertilizing, enriching, and providing
transportation and livelihood, but at times it has also
brought destruction and death. And right in the shadow
of the Great Floodwall, Morgan City's resilient little Main
Street community thrives on optimism and faith, and a
fervent prayer that Mark Twain won't be right after all.

Natchitoches

Population: 18,328

It seems immensely suitable that the oldest permanent European settlement in the Louisiana Purchase should today have one of the most widely praised and loveliest of all downtown Main Street communities. Besides being a feast for the eyes, downtown Natchitoches is a hub of activity, its little shops and businesses bustling and brick-paved Front Street thronged with enthralled tourists. As a small synopsis compiled by the Museum of Historic Natchitoches attests, over the three centuries since its French colonial beginnings, the town has evolved into one of the best examples of the felicitous blending of cultural heritage and economic development.

Natchitoches was founded in 1714 by a French Canadian, Louis Juchereau de St. Denis, whose diplomatic skills as commandant contributed to its early survival. The fort was erected to protect this increasingly vital trade center and to control Spanish incursions from the province of Texas into French Louisiana. Conversely the Spanish, not far to the west, erected their own presidio to keep the French out of Texas. The French garrison initially

was called Fort St. Jean Baptiste, and a fine replica of it, now a state historic site staffed by costumed interpreters, was constructed in the 1970s using detailed eighteenth-century drawings and tools.

French and Spanish trappers, traders, and soldiers came to the area. As the canebrakes along the riverbanks were cleared for small farms and plantations growing indigo, tobacco, and then cotton, Anglo-Americans moved down from the East Coast, bringing African slaves to work the fields. Each nationality made its contribution to the history of the area, and in the lonely wilderness outposts some unusual partnerships were struck. Generations of Cane River Creoles exhibit ancestries that harmoniously blend French, Spanish, Native American, and African blood and traditions. The state's "cradle of Creole culture," they call it still.

From the Natchitoches Indians, part of the Caddo Confederation, the settlement took its name (pronounced NAK-a-tish), and as the area passed from French to Spanish to American control, development expanded from the fort to what is now the center of the Main Street community, Rue Front, along the banks of the Red River. Lining Front Street atop the levee today are historic brick buildings, many with lacy iron balconies reminiscent of the Vieux Carré in New Orleans. Indeed, these two communities that are so strikingly similar have both been named National Historic Landmark Districts.

Picturesque Victorian lampposts hung with immense baskets of colorful blooms and tidy walkways lined with inviting benches brighten this thirty-three-block area

Above: Front Street
Opposite page: Front Street as seen from the levee

year-round. They highlight its unique boutique shops, fine restaurants, cozy saloons, the quintessential indie bookstore—complete with contented cats snoozing in the sunny storefront window—numerous delightful bed and breakfasts, and some very upscale loft living spaces on upper floors of many of the double-galleried buildings. It's no wonder Natchitoches attracts more than a million visitors a year, many enjoying the guided heritage tours via trolley, horse-drawn carriage, even boat. Natchitoches' historic and cultural district has gained prestigious national recognition as a Great American Main Street, one of the National Trust's Dozen Distinctive Destinations, a

Preserve America Community, and a top retirement haven. Starring as the main setting for homegrown playwright Robert Harling's *Steel Magnolias* didn't hurt, either.

It hasn't always been easy—in the 1970s it was said that a person could toss a quarter down Front Street and not hit a thing—but for generations Natchitoches has benefited from the dedication of scores of hard-working preservationists and cooperative local and national preservation organizations, all determined to interpret and protect the area's past to enhance its present. Their work has been supported by farsighted Main Street managers and enthusiastic city administrations putting together incentive rehab funding grants with tax credits and other

Shops along Front Street

inducements from many sources. With the unique Cane River Creole cotton plantation country just to its south, the Natchitoches area is so rich in preserved treasures that it boasts a comprehensive National Heritage Area, a National Historic Park, six National Historic Landmarks, and a large number of National Register structures, all stitched together by a scenic byway.

Once a thriving antebellum port on the Red River, Natchitoches saw its commerce boom because a thick logjam of fallen trees and debris blocked navigation on the upper Red River, making the town the farthest point upriver steamboat traffic from New Orleans could travel. But by the time Capt. Henry Shreve cleared the Great Raft in the 1830s and opened navigation upstream, the Red River had shifted its flow five miles east, rendering Natchitoches inaccessible to most river traffic and curtailing the town's growth.

The resilient folks in Natchitoches turned this adversity into an advantage, however, by damming the thirty-six-mile-long curve of waterway cut off when the Red swung away from town. This created lovely, languid Cane River Lake, center of life and scene of some of the area's most popular festivals, cleverly designed to keep visitors and locals flocking to the historic downtown throughout the year.

Natchitoches' famous month-long Festival of Lights was begun in 1926 when the head of the city's utility department strung a single strand of ten-watt bulbs along Front Street. It now features hundreds of thousands of Christmas lights and more than one hundred riverbank set

developing new and exciting projects to complement old businesses like the big brick Kaffie-Frederick general mercantile store, which has been in operation since the mid-1800s. The streets ascending from the river above Front Street are filled with historic homes and churches, the fascinating American Cemetery with burials beginning in the 1790s, museums, and the iconic Lasyone's Meat Pie Kitchen, as well as contemporary centers for events and the arts.

Recent additions to the Front Street riverfront include Beau Jardin in the Virginia Baker Park, where waterfalls and flagstone patios provide a photogenic wedding venue behind the historic 1796 Roque House, surely a contributing factor in the naming of Natchitoches as one of the top five Most Romantic Main Streets in the country

pieces, plus parades, fireworks, arts and crafts, live music, horse-drawn carriage tours, river cruises, and food, all enjoyed by half a million visitors every year. Other events include historic home tours and Mardi Gras parades, the Meat Pie Festival, which celebrates the town's spicy signature dish, the Folk Festival, held in conjunction with Northwestern State University (begun in 1884 as the state Normal School to train teachers, and a great community source of cultural enrichment with performing arts and symphonic programs), the Jazz-R&B and Zydeco festivals, Cookin' on the Cane, monthly Green Markets during growing season, Art along the Bricks, and Bloomin' on the Bricks.

Not content to rest on its laurels, this Main Street community is a continually evolving streetscape, constantly

Old Courthouse Museum and Lasyone's

by the National Trust for Historic Preservation. Just across the street is the large new Louisiana Sports Hall of Fame Museum, and there's also a new multi-story downtown hotel. From Front Street, the view across Cane River Lake reveals oak-shaded boulevards lined with magnificent Queen Anne and Victorian homes whose manicured lawns slope gently down to the riverfront, perfect settings for Easter egg hunts and garden parties.

It is not by accident that so many of the immensely popular festivals take place "on the bricks." Natchitoches treasures its unique history and heritage with a ferocity not to be taken lightly, as Gov. Earl Long found out in 1958 when he sent a highway crew in a misguided attempt to remove the bricks and blacktop historic Front Street. Preservation-minded ladies of the town, members of the newly formed Association for the Preservation of Historic Natchitoches, joined forces and literally lay down in front of the bulldozers. When highway officials frantically phoned for instructions, the governor asked how many women were involved. "Over one hundred," he was told. Uncle Earl capitulated and ordered the dozers turned around for home.

Today picturesque Rue Front, or Front Street, still proudly wears its bricks, and the city-based Natchitoches Main Street program oversees an extensive commercial district revitalization program that sensibly partners with preservation, economic development, and tourism organizations to ensure broad-based support and the funding to encourage not just rehabilitation of historic structures but also the creation of hundreds of new jobs in new business ventures. Since 1993, when Natchitoches officially became a state Main Street Community, the commercial district building vacancy rate, once as high as 65 percent, has dropped to a mere 1 percent, and investment in rehabilitation and restoration in the district, with limited public seed funds encouraging matching private monies, has soared into the millions of dollars.

The underlying premise of the Main Street approach is to encourage economic development within the context of historic preservation in ways appropriate to today's marketplace. One inspiring success story was the historic turn-of-the-century Nakatosh Hotel, vacant and deteriorating for decades until Natchitoches Main Street partnered with the city, the Natchitoches Historic District Development Commission, and the state Division of Historic Preservation to finance its restoration, returning it to its rightful role as a key anchor of the historic commercial district. The hotel now houses businesses on the first floor and a number of upper-story living spaces.

As Richard Moe, president of the National Trust for Historic Preservation, recognized, "The revitalization of Natchitoches is the direct result of the community's unified goal to reestablish its historic commercial district. Natchitoches has made great strides not only by reclaiming its buildings and recruiting new businesses but by promoting its downtown as the heart and soul of the community."

Nakatosh Hotel along Church Street

New Iberia

Population: 30,617

The New Iberia Historic Commercial District won a 2005 *Great American Main Street Award©*, sponsored by the National Trust for Historic Preservation©, for its successful revitalization efforts. About the recipient of this prestigious recognition, the Trust said, "Downtown New Iberia has successfully re-invented itself as a nucleus of culture, commerce, and tourism that actively celebrates its historic heritage." It doesn't get any better than that.

Actually, it *does* get better. Add to the Trust accolades those of native son, part-time resident, and *New York Times* bestselling author James Lee Burke, who calls New Iberia's Main Street one of the most beautiful streets in the Old South or maybe even in the whole country. As Burke's fictional character, bedeviled detective Dave Robicheaux, roams the streets of New Iberia, the descriptions are so vivid that readers smell the climbing roses and wisteria, salivate as the smoke from crab boils drifts across grassy lawns, stumble on sidewalks twisted by the roots of enormous spreading live oaks, and feel the warmth of the

tropical summer sun filtering through the drifts of Spanish moss along Bayou Teche as the dragonflies hang motionless in the hot air and the alligator gars slip through the water like snakes.

Of course neither the National Trust nor the most lyrical crime writer in America could make something out of nothing, and they didn't have to, for New Iberia is rich in history and preserved historic treasures. And its history is different, for this is the only surviving South Louisiana town owing its colonial origins to Spanish rather than French/Creole/Acadian settlers. In the late 1770s Col. Francisco Bouligny recruited sixteen family groups from Malaga in southern Spain to settle in the Attakapas district, and they called their new home *Nueva Iberia.* Earlier, the area had been occupied by Native Americans attracted by its coastal salt domes, since salt was a valued trade commodity.

French, Creole, and Acadian settlers, slaves from Africa or the Caribbean, even some free people of color joined this small group of Malaguenos along Bayou Teche and Spanish Lake. By 1788 there were nearly two hundred residents of New Iberia. After the Louisiana Purchase in 1803, Anglos would arrive and the great Greek Revival houses like Shadows-on-the-Teche would be built. Most of those grand structures were built in the 1830s, but government surveyor Leander Cathcart reported in 1819 that there were already six houses, a general merchandise store, and a saloon at New Iberia, which was becoming a busy commercial connection between New Orleans and the western prairies.

New Iberia was incorporated in 1839. By then, bayou steamers had replaced the early flatboats and keelboats for transporting goods and passengers. As small plantations were subdivided, beginning in 1829, lots were sold in what is now the heart of downtown New Iberia's commercial district, and in 1837 Frederick Henry Duperier donated a portion of his plantation for St. Peter's Catholic Church. The surrounding fields were planted with sugarcane that thrived in the rich soil and semitropical climate. Local orators claimed that Louisiana had the richest soil for the production of sugar, and the Teche country was styled the Sugar Bowl of America.

The flush years of antebellum prosperity along Bayou Teche were followed by sorely trying times. During the Civil War, Federal forces occupied New Iberia as part of the Teche Campaign in the spring of 1863 and again as part of the Great Texas Overland Expedition from the fall of 1863 through the war's end. The postbellum economy was dismal in this agricultural area of cotton and sugarcane plantations, with floods and freezes, labor shortages, deadly yellow fever epidemics, and fires on Main Street in 1870 and 1899 that destroyed half the town's mostly wooden commercial district. This town, like others, learned the hard way about the vulnerability of crowded wooden structures, resulting in rebuilt downtowns featuring brick structures with metal roofs. Several buildings along East Main stand today as fine examples of the artistry of the late-1800s New Iberia brickmasons Aristide and Alfred Etie.

New Iberia was named the seat of government when

Iberia Parish was created in 1868. With the coming of the railroad, the lumber industry fueled an economic rebound, with local sawmills, planing mills, shingle mills, and sash and door factories providing jobs and shipping trainloads of cypress shingles and other materials to Midwest builders. Other factories produced brick, sugar mill machinery, and wooden wagons, and the unpaved Main Street of the early 1900s was busy with buyers and sellers. A promotional booklet from 1898 called New Iberia "a center of culture, wealth and great natural resources, beautiful in itself and with a bright future, the heart of the rich and beautiful Teche country," where sugarcane crops thrived nearly as heartily as did the residents. Said the booklet, "No extremes of climate are known here, no burning suns, no frozen snows, no chilly blizzards are felt; a delightful atmosphere purified by the gulf breezes, 15 miles distant. . . . The number of old people is greater than in other sections of the United States, there seeming to be a special something conducive to long life."

With the opening of the Little Bayou Oil Field near New Iberia in 1917, oil and gas exploration and production, both onshore and off, assumed a major role in the area's economy and spurred the development of the busy Port of Iberia, which today boasts deepwater channel access to the Gulf of Mexico and the Intracoastal Waterway. Following another period of prosperity, the economy took a dive when the oil industry plummeted in the 1980s, taking New Iberia's downtown with it. Businesses closed and a dying Main Street was marked by empty, deteriorating

Opposite page: Bayou Teche

buildings, as in many other small towns across the state.

But in the early 1970s a revitalization project had been started by the local mayor and several downtown property owners, who hired an architect to plan improvements—everything from sidewalks and street lights to a museum and civic center—that could be implemented in stages. Efforts really stepped up in 1994, when a Historic District Commission was organized and the town joined the state Main Street program, building on early preservation and beautification efforts and breathing new life into downtown commercial buildings. Goals included saving historic buildings while reviving the commercial core of downtown and strengthening and diversifying the existing business base, all while maintaining a sense of place and community life.

Millions of dollars in incentive grants and matching funding, plus some very creative initiatives, sparked an exciting resurgence of the downtown area. The nationally recognized Main Street program continually provides encouragement and education on business development and tax incentives for historic renovation as well as grant funding, while recruiting new businesses and utilizing promotional materials to keep the downtown area hopping with locals and tourists alike. Main Street worked with one hesitant developer to turn a large vacant department store space into a mini-mall with retail shops and living and office space, all functioning behind a preserved historic face. It also instigated ordinance changes that allowed restoration of historic commercial structures with over-sidewalk balconies and upper-floor living space, allowing

existing downtown buildings to be used to their fullest potential, the unique upper-story residential development enhancing the possibility of round-the-clock downtown activities.

The New Iberia Main Street program defines itself as "a public/private partnership of people committed to preserving and enhancing our downtown's economy by attracting local residents and visitors to celebrate our diverse culture and enjoy our natural and historic resources." Its achievements exemplify the overall Main Street approach to revitalization of commercial districts and preservation of historic structures. Before and after images of the downtown district clearly show an area taken from dull and deteriorating to vibrant and exciting, with colorful landscaping, increased parking, adaptive architectural preservation, and additional residential and retail space, all providing a happy marriage of cultural charm with vibrant commerce and tourism opportunities. Street signs are now trilingual in a tip of the hat to New Iberia's unique heritage.

Since 1994, New Iberia's downtown has gained more than one hundred new businesses, hundreds of new jobs, and millions of dollars in private investments, with wonderful restaurants—Little River Inn; Clementine for fine dining; Pelicans, which is accessible by boat; BoJangles Sushi and Oyster Bar; Victor's Cafeteria, so dear to the heart of James Lee Burke and home of the world's best pralines and crawfish pies; the charming café-style ambience of Lagniappe Too; and others—boutique specialty shops, the state-of-the-art Bayou Teche Museum with interactive

children's gallery and changing exhibits on local history, historic churches, and a variety of vital business and service offices, right on the banks of Bayou Teche and connected by a scenic boardwalk along the tranquil waterway. Splendid bed and breakfast accommodations are available, including Bayou Teche Guest Cottage, Estorge-Norton House, and Le Rosier Country Inn. The brick walls and tin roof of the 1893 Gouguenheim served as a fire break in the 1899 conflagration.

The National Register-listed East Main Street Historic District in this "Queen City of the Teche" is a three-quarter-mile section with more than seventy structures dating from the late 1800s and early 1900s. East Main Street is the commercial end of the street, while West Main, a charming boulevard lined with ancient live oaks

shading dozens of picturesque historic homes as well as the Civic Center and library, is primarily residential. The walking tour maps of each end of the street, available at the Iberia Parish Convention and Visitors Bureau Welcome Center, provide architecturally colorful descriptions of each wonderful home, ranging from Colonial Revival or Queen Anne Revival to Greek Revival and Steamboat Gothic, even "vaguely Romanesque." The home of James Lee Burke's grandfather is called a "one-and-a-half story brick ersatz medieval manor house."

The dividing line between residential and commercial Main Streets is the glorious National Historic Landmark called Shadows-on-the-Teche, built between 1831 and 1834 by planter David Weeks. Its architectural style is Classical Revival, with concessions to the semitropical climate like the exterior stairs, wide galleries, upstairs living quarters, and carefully planned cross-ventilation. Eight enormous Tuscan columns cross the front of the red brick structure, which is so well insulated from busy Main Street by a thick bamboo curtain that the grounds offer a splendid serenity; the rear lawns slope down to the bayou. Weeks' widow and children were living in the home when it was commandeered by Union troops as headquarters during the Civil War, and when his wife died in 1863, she had to be buried in her gardens because "the graveyards were all open, the fencing having been torn down by the Yankees."

The home remained in the family for four generations; the last occupant was Weeks Hall, an artistic character who entertained famous guests and agonized over the

Shadows-on-the-Teche

future of his fragile home, recognizing that "the Path of Progress is every bit as destructive as the Path of Decay." Just prior to his death, word was received that his beloved Shadows had been accepted as a National Trust for Historic Preservation property and would be properly interpreted and enjoyed by visitors in perpetuity. Today the Trust welcomes more than twenty-five thousand visitors annually to what is not so much a house tour as an immersion in the very essence of history in a home full of original family furnishings, portraits, textiles, and carefully preserved documentation, some seventeen thousand documents in all. On the beautifully landscaped two-and-a-half-acre grounds, educational history camps for children, arts and crafts festivals, Easter egg hunts, garden strolls, Christmas Merry-Making Season, and Civil War reenactments involve the community throughout the year in programs designed to encourage an appreciation of historic preservation through fun activities.

Just beyond the Shadows' bamboo curtain, the rest of the bustling downtown historic district, besides being busy and beautiful, also knows how to have fun. The Essanee Theater, which opened in 1937 and ran films until 1985, now houses the Iberia Performing Arts League. The Sliman Theater for the Performing Arts began life as a wholesale grocery in the late nineteenth century, then enjoyed popularity as an Art Deco movie theater called the Evangeline. Donated to the City of New Iberia in 1994 and listed on the National Register of Historic Places, the Sliman's restored facilities serve as a multipurpose cultural center, the setting for theatrical performances

The Evangeline Theater, now the Sliman Theater for the Performing Arts

and concerts, and a space for private functions. Both of these facilities benefitted from Main Street façade grants.

Special events bring even more folks to the bayouside to enjoy James Lee Burke's favorite Main Street (there are even walking and driving tours designed to point out locations mentioned—with a little literary license—in Burke's books, and at least one of his books has been turned into a movie filmed in part in New Iberia, with lots of local participation). Most of New Iberia's festivals feature plenty of great food and Cajun or Zydeco music for dancing in this area noted for its traditional *joie de vivre*. Several times a year, the Main Street program joins with the New Iberia Arts and Cultural Commission to host New Iberia Downtown Artwalk, which displays the works of more than a hundred artists throughout the historic area's retail spaces, restaurants, and professional offices, plus live music in the gazebo at Bouligny Plaza and book signings at the wonderful little indie bookstore called Books Along the Teche (when James Lee Burke autographs his latest releases there, as he always does, the waiting lines go clear around the block). The Teche Area Farmers' Market at Bouligny Plaza is open bi-weekly year-round. The Gumbo Cook-off, Cajun Fun Fest, and exuberant Louisiana Sugar Cane Festival (begun in 1941) celebrate New Iberia's cultural heritage, and holidays like Mardi Gras, the Fourth of July, and Christmas are marked by parades and special events (Yuletide on the Bayou involves hundreds of Girl Scouts designing and building gingerbread houses for display in downtown storefronts). The Bunk Johnson Jazz Festival recalls the famous 1920s jazz trumpeter who is buried in New Iberia. One of the great New Orleans musicians, he was touring with the Black Eagle band in Rayne in 1931 when a fight cost him his front teeth and his trumpet, necessitating a break in his musical career while he did manual labor until fellow musicians pitched in to buy dentures and a new trumpet, reviving his career for another decade.

New Iberia's Conrad Rice Mill and its wonderful country store offer local products and tastings. In what is called America's oldest operating rice mill, visitors watch the fascinating process that for a century has taken rice grains from field to package. Besides being part of America's Wetland Birding Trail, New Iberia is on both the Bayou Teche and Jean Lafitte Scenic Byway drives that wind through Cajun and Creole country, passing sugarcane fields and fine plantation homes along sleepy bayous, where drivers catch just a hint of briny Gulf breezes. Featured destinations near New Iberia include cypress-studded Lake Fausse Point and Spanish Lake; the world-famous Avery Island, home of Tabasco (because of which they promote this as the HOT side of the Atchafalaya National Heritage Area) and bird rookeries in Jungle Gardens; Jefferson Island, with its Rip Van Winkle Gardens and the Joseph Jefferson House; and the Jeanerette Museum, with its exhibits on the history of the area sugarcane industry. There are guided swamp tours, plus superb fishing and boating in inland lakes and Gulf waters.

But consider what a visitor to Shadows-on-the-Teche wrote, in the later years of Weeks Hall's life: "Why should Weeks Hall ever die? He has his heaven right here." That goes for the rest of New Iberia's Main Street as well; why indeed should anyone have to go anywhere else?

New Orleans

New Orleans—the Big Easy, the Land of Dreamy Dreams—faced unprecedented challenges following the devastation of Hurricane Katrina and the ensuing flooding of much of the city in 2005. Widespread death and destruction, followed by the diaspora of thousands of surviving residents (many of whom never returned), left sections of New Orleans filled with blight—overgrown lots where houses once stood, damaged properties untouched since the storm, ubiquitous blue tarps covering shattered rooftops, large populations of homeless people, and abandoned dogs, cats, and a surprisingly large population of chickens gone wild.

And yet, thanks to a change in municipal government and a national outpouring of support from hundreds of organized programs and thousands of individual volunteers, many parts of the city have struggled back, some even better than before. The state and national Main Street programs have helped by including not just historic small-town downtowns, but also some commercial corridors running through large urban centers, permitting access to funding and support services to help rebuild the economic and social vitality of a handful of core neighborhoods within the Crescent City. Hence New Orleans has within its boundaries several distinct urban districts that are identified as Main Street communities, each a unique area building on its specific cultural assets, each basically a single street.

North Rampart Street

This district is comprised of thirteen blocks stretching from Canal Street to Esplanade Avenue; a third of its area is owned by the city. It is called the gateway to the French Quarter, just a few blocks from Jackson Square and the iconic attractions of the Vieux Carré. During Hurricane Katrina, part of the district flooded and all of it received heavy wind damage, but it has made—and continues to make—a remarkable recovery.

The highlight of the recovery effort is the Saenger Theatre on Canal, built in 1927 at a cost of $2.5 million, with an admission price of sixty-five cents to a program of silent movies, stage plays, and orchestral music. It was designed by architect Emile Weil to evoke the feeling of an Italian baroque courtyard, with special ceiling lights duplicating the constellations. Designated a historic landmark by the New Orleans Landmark Commission and listed on the National Register of Historic Places, the theater underwent a $3 million renovation into a performing arts center in 1978, but suffered significant water damage as a result of Hurricane Katrina in 2005. The waterline reached a foot above the stage level. In 2009 a unique partnership between the Canal Street Development Corporation (a city agency) and the Saenger Theatre Partnership Ltd.

made it possible to secure the $38.8 million required for restoration through a combination of federal grants, state and federal tax credits, and private financing.

While the Saenger underwent restoration, its scheduled Broadway productions were staged at the Mahalia Jackson Theatre for the Performing Arts. Named for iconic gospel singer and New Orleans native Mahalia Jackson, this theater is located in the thirty-two-acre Louis Armstrong Park toward the Esplanade Avenue

their culture. A statue honors New Orleans' beloved Louis Armstrong, and, appropriately, this park was the first site of the New Orleans Jazz & Heritage Festival.

North Rampart Street is a colorful blend of light industrial and wholesale businesses, a few restaurants and bars, some churches and shelters, a wonderfully renovated multi-building courtyard hotel called the French Quarter Suites, the studios of WWL, and the Jazz and Heritage Building, which uses an old funeral parlor as a music school. Another iconic music site is the first recording studio of Cosimo Matassa; the structure dates from 1835, and it was there the New Orleans sound developed from pioneering R&B and rock and roll legends like Fats Domino, Professor Longhair, Little Richard, Jerry Lee Lewis, and Ray Charles. Tax incentives and grants

Above: Jazz and Heritage Building
Opposite page: Congo Square

end of the North Rampart Street district, bordering the Tremé neighborhood. With a seating capacity of 2,100, it has featured performances by the Louisiana Philharmonic Orchestra, New Orleans Ballet Association, New Orleans Opera Association, New Orleans Jazz Orchestra, and Broadway Across America touring productions. Besides the Mahalia Jackson Theater, Armstrong Park contains the New Orleans Municipal Auditorium, part of the New Orleans Jazz National Historical Park, and the site of Congo Square, where enslaved and free African-Americans gathered on Sunday afternoons in the eighteenth and early nineteenth centuries to drum and sing, trade, and dance the Bamboula and the Calinda in an effort to preserve

are encouraging the repopulation of this corridor, with projects like the renovation of an old furniture store into condominiums whose price tags range from $250,000 to $4 million.

The neutral ground, restored after Katrina with fresh palm trees and attractive light standards, is being prepared for an extension of the streetcar line that will bring even more interest here. New Orleans' famous streetcars once reached most corners of the city, but in recent years the lines have run mostly in the area upriver from the French Quarter. Current plans to rerun streetcars to Downtown and into more working-class Creole areas are a promising sign, says journalist Cain Burdeau, that New Orleans is reinventing itself by restoring its past.

Pres Kabacoff is an innovative developer who has made huge investments in reinvigorating New Orleans' St. Claude Avenue corridor and other historic neighborhoods across the country, and he says it's about time. "We have spent a lot of time in the last hundred years paying attention to Uptown New Orleans," he says. "The opportunity the city has now is Downtown." And the extension of the streetcar line down Rampart Street and St. Claude, according to one local hotelier, will be a welcome driver of connectivity, convenience, and historic authenticity.

Rehab projects have yielded some pleasant surprises

here; what the Main Street manager described as the ugliest building on the street was stripped of its outer layer to reveal wonderful 1840s brick, and a rushed and severely botched repair job done to Armstrong Park is being rectified. Thanks to hard-working property owners, businesses, and preservationists, with help from Main Street grants to structures like St. Marks United Methodist Church, and with a dynamic Main Street manager so determined that she even conducted tours for visiting professionals while sporting casts on not one but two broken wrists, the North Rampart Street neighborhood is now vibrant and healthy, and attractive as well.

O. C. Haley Boulevard

The Main Street approach to revitalizing commercial districts involves leveraging local assets, from cultural and architectural heritage to local enterprises and community pride. Business districts must capitalize on the assets that make them unique, qualities like distinctive buildings and the human scale that provide a sense of community and give residents a real sense of belonging to that community. The O. C. Haley Main Street district provides a prime example of just that.

Originally known as Dryades Street, the boulevard was renamed in the 1980s for Central City resident Mrs. Oretha Castle Haley, a civil rights pioneer who founded the New Orleans chapter of Congress of Racial Equality. Two blocks from St. Charles Avenue between the lower Garden District and the Central Business District, the area was once a thriving mecca for New Orleans' African American and immigrant communities. Jewish immigrants arrived in the nineteenth century, selling wares first from push carts, then stalls, and finally stores that welcomed the black patrons who were not permitted to try on clothing in other neighborhoods. The Dryades Street Market was the center of the commercial district. It was home to nightclubs and the city's first black public library, the Carnegie Library.

Today the area is a New Orleans Urban Main Street and cultural and commercial district in Central City. Rehabilitation and repopulation there focuses on a celebration of African-American culture, history, and commerce, and the entire planning process emphasizes Afro-Caribbean arts and the resistance movement of its civil rights heritage. One cultural anchor of the district is the Ashe Cultural Arts Center, situated in an old

Ashe Cultural Arts Center

department store building. Co-founder Carol Bebelle saw the center's purpose as providing accessible facilities for emerging or established artists and other culture bearers to use art and culture to foster human development, civic engagement, and economic justice in the African-American community. By combining the intentions of neighborhood and economic development with the creative forces of community culture and art, the center has helped revive and reclaim this historically significant corridor in Central City.

This "Renaissance on the Boulevard" uses storytelling, poetry, music, dance, photography, and visual art to revive the area's possibilities, providing performance space, dance and recording studios, meeting and workshop rooms, a

Café Reconcile

catering kitchen, exhibit space, and a locale for a variety of community cultural and educational programs for all ages. A repertoire of original theater works is available for touring, and many of the community workshops emphasize healthy lifestyle changes in enjoyable programs like the exercise/dance programs combining African, second lining, salsa, hip hop and other moves for participants from age two to eighty-six. With affordable lofts and office space upstairs, Ashe provides a community space and gathering spot. It has hosted everything from weddings to funerals.

Another anchor is the old Handelman's Department Store, now Non-Profit Central, which played an especially important role matching needs with resources as a clearinghouse for non-profits in the aftermath of Katrina. HOPE Community Credit provides financial advice and assistance for residents and business owners. Café Reconcile is a neighborhood restaurant that provides at-risk kids with training in life and work skills in the hospitality and construction industries, its culinary component now partnering with famous New Orleans chefs Emeril Lagasse and John Besh. This program, lovingly called "the kitchen of life," is a three-week inspirational job-training and esteem-building regimen that aspires to save young people from the cycle of poverty and violence plaguing their neighborhoods. It has been so successful that it serves 150 lunches a day and is renovating its five-story building.

One exciting development near Café Reconcile is the reclamation of part of the old Dryades Street Market, one of dozens of neighborhood markets operated by the city in the late 1800s. The fascinating Southern Food and

Beverage Museum, opened in the Riverwalk Marketplace to showcase Louisiana's rich culinary history, hopes by 2013 to move into this 30,000-square-foot historic structure on O. C. Haley Boulevard. This move will give the museum much more space; there will be two floors of displays, galleries and exhibits, plus a kitchen auditorium, children's gallery, restaurant, and bar. The museum will partner with a Washington, D.C., real estate development firm, Thoron, whose president Robert Taylor calls the project a major investment in the community and envisions the museum as anchor tenant in the development of several mixed-use sites in the neighborhood, including the Gators Building, "focused on bringing a mixture of uses, spaces to live, work, play, dine and learn."

When O. C. Haley Boulevard became a Main Street District in 2006, twenty-three of the fifty listed properties were vacant, and there were only nine street-level retail spaces. Today this district is a prime example of the benefits of owning and celebrating cultural heritage. Streetscape improvements, markers on significant landmarks, a planned State Civil Rights Institute, special events, and enhanced street lighting will soon make the boulevard an even more inviting urban environment.

O. C. Haley Boulevard

St. Claude Avenue

Located in the Upper Ninth Ward, St. Claude Avenue suffered severe damage from levee and floodwall failures during Hurricane Katrina. The commercial corridor here, its small businesses interspersed with residences, traditionally served the historic neighborhoods of Bywater, lower Marigny, and St. Roch. When much of its customer base was dispersed by the hurricane, the area, already damaged by the storm, deteriorated even further. Urban blight marked the streetscape; the few structures being restored were interspersed with abandoned buildings propped up by two-by-fours.

As one local business owner put it, "This area fell on hard times and lost many family businesses. It became known as Furniture Row, the place to come to buy cheap mattresses." But as one door closed, another opened. "Cheap" became the operative word in creating a unique context that attracted small start-up businesses and courageous creative artists drawn by inexpensive rental and purchase prices for property. Once the seed of an art community was planted, galleries, studios, and related small businesses began to provide infinitely more appeal than cheap mattresses.

The Shadow Box Theatre, where squatters had once camped with extension cords plugged into the utility box, is now a small theater company. There are ambitious plans to restore the historic St. Roch Market building, once a popular seafood market for the city of New Orleans. Efforts like the Green Project, which recycles architectural elements and encourages environmental consciousness, and a food co-op, begun when the area did

St. Roch Market building

not have grocery stores after the storm, fit right in with other small businesses locating to structures rehabbed with a cooperative, creative community in mind.

Dozens of studios and galleries provide outlets for homegrown cutting-edge art, and Main Street fosters the development of the area as an arts/destination cluster by connecting interested occupants and businesses with empty spaces. Investors and property owners are restoring structures, keeping preservation and affordable rent to small businesses in mind, and bold eye-catching colors are replacing unattractive metal slipcovers on many buildings. Bertie's is a good example. A warm and welcoming coffee house/art gallery established by a lively former limo driver, it also provides exhibit space for the mosaic creations of the late Giovanni Coserra, whose artwork was rescued from a

flooded home in the neighborhood.

Another innovative and ambitious multi-use project is the New Orleans Healing Center, 55,000 square feet of the abandoned landmark Universal Furniture store that has been adaptively and attractively restored to house artists and collectives, a vodou botanica, a grocery co-op, performance space, yoga and dance studios, an organic restaurant and juice bar, a fitness center, and a variety of other eclectic tenants that spill over into the building next door. Developers/partners Pres Kabacoff and Sally Ann Glassman insisted that participants in this ambitious experiment had to be not just financially sustainable, but spiritually sustainable as well, capable of bringing together a diverse population in a transformative way while stimulating the economic development of the area. With investment by the National Trust Community Investment Corporation—the tax credit syndicator subsidiary of the National Trust for Historic Preservation—the New

New Orleans Healing Center

Orleans Healing Center hopes to become a worldwide model for urban community healing. To enlighten and engage, to be culturally aware, to respect the environment and to provide economic possibilities, to *heal*: isn't that exactly what restoration and revitalization must do for a broken and blighted community?

Nearby, in the Lower Ninth Ward, abandoned structures untouched since Katrina still bear the spray-painted inspection records showing dates and number of bodies. Yet even in that devastated area there are pockets of hope—Katrina cottages, the innovative designs of Brad Pitt's Make It Right foundation, and Musicians' Village, spearheaded by Harry Connick, Jr.

Most hopeful for the St. Claude commercial corridor are plans to extend streetcar lines from the French Quarter east down Rampart Street and St. Claude Avenue, connecting busy Canal Street with the neighborhoods of Tremé, Marigny, New Marigny, St. Roch, and the Bywater, areas said to have rarely been considered major tourist destinations in spite of their undeniable historic relevance and unique cultural heritages. As Mayor Mitch Landrieu enthusiastically told AP journalist Cain Burdeau, "We fully expect the presence of this rail line will have a catalytic effect. It doesn't just move people, it also creates economic development. It fits with our culture, it fits with our history." "Transit lines add value and desirability to property in an area," said Chris Leinberger, visiting fellow with the Metropolitan Policy Program at the Brookings Institution, addressing Louisiana's annual Smart Growth conference in 2011. "You put a streetcar line down there, and you will get high-quality development," he said.

St. Claude Avenue Urban Main Street, with its rehab incentive grants and other programs, strives to cultivate, nurture, and sustain an economic revival of this historic commercial district, leveraging private improvements while making revitalization efforts affordable and community-based. Reversing the "broken-window syndrome" with building rehabilitation improves safety, walk-ability, and business opportunity, attracts customers and additional businesses, and improves the quality of life for residents and visitors alike.

Charles Colton Public School

Broad Street

At eighteen blocks, Broad Street is the longest corridor in the New Orleans Main Street urban districts program, but it is also a state highway, old Hwy. 90 that was part of the Old Spanish Trail traversing the high ground of the Gentilly Ridge and connecting via Bayou Road to the Native American portage trail that led the earliest explorers and settlers to the French Quarter without having to brave the dangerous mouth of the Mississippi River from the Gulf. The sheer length of the corridor presents both a challenge and an opportunity.

Broad Street is one of New Orleans' most heavily travelled roadways, with over forty thousand cars passing every day. There are more than one hundred small businesses along this busy corridor, most—cafes and bars, automotive service shops, barbershops and hair salons, book and record stores—providing routine services and goods for the surrounding neighborhoods. Broad Street Main Street also includes several Louisiana Cultural Districts where properties are eligible for state tax credits and original art purchases are exempt from state sales tax. Many of its structures are mid-century modern, not the antebellum grandeur as seen in other neighborhoods.

And that's just fine with the residents and small business

owners along this corridor. David McGee, a technician at Pumping Station Number 2 on the Broad Street neutral ground, grew up in this area and remembers it as full of life, with no vacant storefronts; Broad Street was even traversed by the Endymion parade during Mardi Gras. He doesn't want to let go of the soul of that old neighborhood. "You want to see the street revitalized," he admits, "but you don't want to lose what makes it New Orleans. And what makes it New Orleans is the people. . . . If you had

total gentrification, you'd lose the pulse and the feeling of the street itself."

McGee and others share their stories in a wonderful multimedia exploration called *Who's On Broad*, an intriguing collaboration between the Who's On Broad Story Project and the University of New Orleans Department of Planning and Urban Studies–Main Street Task Force. McGee's passion for preserving the old neighborhood's heart and soul is a sentiment with which the Broad Street Main Street program is in total accord.

Broad Community Connections (BCC) is the name of the non-profit Main Street organization established after Hurricane Katrina. Its stated purpose is to bring new life, commerce, and opportunity to Broad Street between Tulane Avenue and Bayou Road, and it partners with a wide variety of organizations—Keep Louisiana Beautiful, The Phoenix of New Orleans, Tulane University, Friends of Lafitte Corridor, and Providence Community Housing, among others—to carry out that mission in ways appropriate to the heritage and history of the area.

In 2007 a comprehensive plan was developed for Broad Street with assistance from a graduate class in the Department of Urban Studies and Planning at MIT, from which institution the passionate young BCC director, a New Orleans native, just happens to have a Masters in City Planning. Included in the planning process for this revitalization strategy were numerous neighborhood residents, community organizations, and business owners, all with an interest in restoring vitality to this historic commercial corridor.

Side streets off of Broad offer glimpses of colorful cottages.

BCC considers its Broad Street corridor a microcosm of the Crescent City, its diverse threads integral to the fabric of New Orleans and its rhythms the rhythms of the city. The surrounding neighborhoods contribute incredible diversity: Tremé, Faubourg St. John, Esplanade Ridge, Bayou Road, Mid-City, and Lower Mid-City. BCC strives to bring together these ethnically varied neighborhoods and foster their economic, residential, and cultural development, all the while retaining respect for their unique identities.

And what incredible diversity there is! Broad Street is the frontline of New Orleans' pumping system. The street is home to the headquarters of the Zulu Social Aide and Pleasure Club, New Orleans' largest mostly African

American carnival organization. Liberty's Kitchen is an unpretentious café providing training in culinary and life skills for at-risk youth today, but the original high-dollar Ruth's Chris Steak House was here, continuing a tradition begun at Crescent City Steaks with John Vojkoich in 1934.

The wonderful Gothic Revival frame church now home to the Victory Fellowship congregation was founded in 1918 as the Immanuel Evangelical Lutheran Church by German immigrants. The large numbers of German immigrants who settled in New Orleans were also responsible for the long history of beer brewing in the city, beginning in the mid-1800s. The brewery district

Originally Immanuel Evangelical Lutheran Church

was centered at Broad and Tulane when New Orleans was known as the Queen City of Brewing; Dixie and Falstaff Brewery buildings still stand. One of the Main Street program's most popular events is the Broad Street Brewhaha, a rooftop sampling of microbrewery products in celebration of New Orleans' coffee and beer-brewing traditions. Other special events include flea markets and fresh markets designed to invigorate the area and increase awareness of its charms.

A proposed linear park called the Lafitte Greenway will cross Broad between Lafitte and St. Louis streets, connecting the French Quarter with City Park and incorporating the old Carondelet Canal and Southern Railways corridors into what will be the first new park in New Orleans in twenty years. Streetscape enhancements

include landscaping, signage, sidewalks, lighting, and bike lanes to create a more pedestrian- and family-friendly corridor while enhancing commercial development along Broad.

Enormous medical construction projects are taking place in the area, including the controversial new Veterans Administration/Tulane-LSU-Xavier facility replacing Charity Hospital for healthcare, medical training, and research. A new Tulane Medical School community

health center, new biosciences institutions, and research consortiums will have a huge impact on the Broad Street area, raising demands for shopping, services, and housing. The Lafitte Housing Development is being reconfigured as an innovative mixed-income community, and BCC hopes to capitalize on the new medical developments in ways that will not destroy its historic neighborhoods.

The program on Broad is one of the more recent state Main Street communities, but this is an area that will change and develop enormously, and in very short order, with all the multi-million dollar construction projects in the vicinity. Can Broad Street retain its historic heart and soul, as David McGee hopes, while embracing new life, new opportunities, and economic vitality? It can if BCC has anything to do with it, for the very name—Broad Community Connections—of the Main Street program here implies that one of its major goals is promoting neighborhood ownership, encouraging and supporting a sense of ownership and pride on Broad Street. This is indeed a connected community, a true neighborhood, and its property owners, businesses, and residents are working to enhance the present and create new promise for the future while building on their unique and rich heritage and history.

New Roads

Population: 4,831

The story of New Roads is the tale of two rivers: one real, one false. The rivers were once connected to each other, and New Roads was intimately connected to them both. Still is.

In 1699, Pierre LeMoyne, Sieur d'Iberville, ascended the Mississippi River to take possession of the Mississippi Valley in the name of King Louis XIV of France. The expedition was advised by Native American guides to make use of a detour via a six-foot-wide creek that bypassed a great bend in the river, saving a day's journey. This same shortcut might well have been used as early as the spring of 1682 by LaSalle, whose party became the first Europeans to descend the Mississippi.

At any rate, the Mississippi River itself soon took advantage of this same short cut in its never-ending quest for the shortest, straightest route to the Gulf, cutting off a twenty-two-mile-long bend that came to be known as *Fausse Rivière*, False River. The surrounding parish was given the name *Pointe Coupée*, meaning "cut point" in French, and the oxbow lake was eventually separated from the main channel of the river except in times of flood. Said

old river pilot Mark Twain in *Life on the Mississippi*, "The Mississippi is remarkable . . . its disposition to make prodigious jumps by cutting through narrow necks of land, and thus straightening and shortening itself."

Pointe Coupée would become one of the first permanent settlements in the Mississippi Valley, the census of 1727 counting eighteen men, seven women, and four children, all French. By the following year, the first Catholic baptism was recorded, baby Jean Francois Decoux. To protect these colonial settlers, a small military redoubt was built (and later greatly expanded), and by 1731 the population had swelled to fifty-five French men, women, and children, plus fifty-six slaves (most of them African, a few Native Americans).

In 1738 the first church was established, St. Francis of Pointe Coupée, and the first small levees were erected to protect from river floodwaters the fields where tobacco and indigo were planted, along with corn and other food crops. By the 1745 census the settlement had grown considerably, with 260 Europeans, 391 African slaves, 20 Native American slaves, 15 mulatto slaves, and 3 free Native Americans, plus 86 horses, 854 cows, and 292 hogs. More than 1,700 arpents of land were under cultivation at the time, mostly along the Mississippi, but by the mid-1700s settlement was beginning in earnest along False River as well. A *chemin neuf* or "new road" connecting settlement along the Mississippi with the newly settled lands along False River gave its name to the town that developed there.

These figures are quoted from resident historian Brian Costello's comprehensive *A History of Pointe Coupée Parish, Louisiana*. Costello also notes that, while the earliest French settlers were eventually joined by African slaves, Spanish immigrants, and—mostly after the Louisiana Purchase—Anglo-Americans, there were no Acadians, primarily because Spanish Governor Ulloa allowed those exiles to populate more southerly unsettled areas. New Roads' location was about the uppermost apex of the geographical and cultural French triangle of South Louisiana, and police jury records and newspapers continued to be printed at least partially in French well after the Civil War.

Toward the end of the 1700s, the great galleried Creole plantations of Pointe Coupée began to be built; remarkably, some still exist today, most notably Parlange. Vincent de Ternant of Parlange, Dr. Benjamin Farrar, Joseph and Antoine Decuir of Austerlitz and River Lake Plantations, and others (French, Anglo, and Creoles of color) began amassing great properties and living rather royally, or so it would seem from the 1792 inventory of the estate of Jean Claude Trenonay, which included a table service of 47 pieces of silver, 503 faience plates, 86 cups, 72 glasses, 40 tablecloths, and a rather astonishing 644 napkins. An early traveler through the region, C. C. Robin, described the area in an account published in Paris in 1807: "The tables are served with a European research which is astonishing in these countries so far away." When Vincent de Ternant's son died in 1842, his estate included 371 pieces of china and 75 wine and champagne glasses, and *his* son's succession inventory mentioned 139 pieces of

silver flatware, bespeaking a flair for gracious entertaining that continues unabated at Parlange today.

Another notable early landowner in Pointe Coupée was Julien Poydras, who began purchasing property in the area in 1775 and entertained the Duc d'Orleans, later King Louis Philippe of France, on one of his plantations in the area in 1798. After the Louisiana Purchase in 1803, Pointe Coupée was one of the original twelve officially established parishes, with Julien Poydras as its first civil commandant and the abandoned military post serving as the location of its first courthouse.

As cotton and sugarcane began to be cultivated on a large scale in the area, Poydras stood out as one of the wealthiest planters in 1807, owning eight large tracts of land and more than 250 slaves (whose emancipation was included in his will, though never actually carried out). He also enjoyed enormous respect as a merchant, banker, and philanthropist. Pres. Thomas Jefferson appointed Poydras to the Territory of Orleans Legislature, where he was instrumental in establishing the state's first public schools in Pointe Coupée. He would subsequently serve in Congress and as president of the Louisiana Constitutional Convention as the state went through the process leading to statehood in 1812. Born in France where he was unable to marry his sweetheart whose family was too poor to provide a dowry, Poydras never married, and in his will he left an endowment for local brides, "the unfortunate always to be preferred."

In 1822 the town of New Roads was begun when Catherine Depau, free woman of color, subdivided twenty lots from her plantation along False River. Adjoining this tract, in 1822 widowed Marie Pourciau Robillard Olinde provided space for the construction of St. Mary's Church. A few houses and shops were constructed, soon to be joined by more stores, hotels, coffeehouses, and the shops of cobblers and tailors. A new courthouse and jail, built for an initial estimate of $14,000, were erected in 1847–48.

Mississippi River steamboats and smaller lake steamers connected Pointe Coupée and New Roads to the outside world, permitting shipment of cotton and cane crops to commission merchants in New Orleans and allowing passenger travel as well as the importation of supplies. By

Looking across the railroad tracks, New Roads 1938. *Russell Lee, Farm Security Administration.*

the 1850s, New Roads bustled with businesses servicing the plantation economy: attorneys, carpenters, clerks, coopers, physicians, bakers, barkeeps, shoemakers, merchants, and bricklayers (many of the latter members of the growing group of exceptionally skilled Creoles of color). Some of the homes constructed in town in the 1830s—Mon Reve, Samson House (now a fine bed and breakfast), and Lejeune House—are still there today.

J. W. Dorr in the 1860 *New Orleans Crescent* called New Roads "quite a pleasant place, loosely scattered along the water's edge; and, indeed, it is hard to tell where settlement ends and the country proper begins, so thickly settled is the coast all round its circuit." The congregation flocked to St. Mary's Church on the banks of False River "in carriages, on horseback and in rowboats and sailboats via 'the river'." When the disastrous 1882 flooding of the Mississippi River put four feet of water on Main Street and five feet in St. Mary's Cemetery, Mrs. Philogene Langlois' funeral procession had to proceed by boat and her remains were entombed in the uppermost vault.

The Civil War brought soldiers and scavengers from both sides into the parish, and the aftermath was dismal. An 1881 issue of the *Pointe Coupée Banner* said, "How destructive the war was can be readily understood when it is remembered that this was a border parish, alternately occupied by first one and then by the other of the contending forces." After the war, there remained "not a house in decent repair, either in New Roads or within five miles of it—there was not a good fence, not a single steam gin, no supply of good work stock, and only a few

Downtown New Roads

broken-down old mules and Creole ponies." In short, it was "a desolate place and an impoverished people." And yet, the *Banner* continued optimistically, "Under all of these disadvantages this people went to work cheerfully to try and build up the country and their fortunes."

New Roads was incorporated as a town in 1875 and again in 1894. By the turn of the century, with the coming of the railroad, it became an important commercial and industrial center. Costello records, "By 1905, new one-and two-story buildings sporting wooden porches and balconies had risen shoulder-to-shoulder along either side of Main Street in New Roads. The five-block stretch between St. Mary's Church and the Courthouse still contained a couple of residences, but most of the available space was taken up by retail stores, pharmacies, hotels, saloons, and the offices of attorneys, physicians and dentists." There were dry-goods emporiums, grocers, hardware stores, and banks. Large Victorian homes went up along East and West Main, and the earliest wooden sidewalks were laid along a section of Main Street. The town streets were dirt thoroughfares until 1919, when Main Street and others were graveled, and it wasn't until the roads were paved in the 1930s that at least some horse-drawn vehicles ceased to be utilized.

The exact center of Louisiana's population until 2000, Pointe Coupée developed as a place of odd juxtapositions: French but not Cajun, rich plantation mansions beside petite Creole cabins, it's the area where the dominant sugarcane crop of South Louisiana began to be supplanted by the cotton crop of the Delta and northern fields. In the late nineteenth century, travel writer Martha R. Fields wrote in the *New Orleans Daily Picayune,* "It is here that the cotton and the sugarcane meet, and often the wind lifts the long snowy banners from the one field and loops them, frayed and featherlight, on the purple scepters of the other. It is here the smokes of the cotton gin and sugar mill marry in the sky. And it is here the grand plantation home stands beside, but dares not encroach upon, the modest domain of the simple French peasant farmer, whose father's father's father had these wooly and canestruck acres in a grant from a foreign king."

Today Pointe Coupée remains primarily rural, its predominant crops sugarcane, cotton, soybeans, and cattle. The area remains a top pecan producer; in the 1940s the

Parlange

late H. J. Bergeron opened a pecan shelling and shipping operation that continues to this day. During the 1970s, oil and gas discoveries in the Tuscaloosa Trend brought a taste of prosperity to the area.

A number of historic plantation homes remain, although only the incredible National Historic Landmark home called Parlange, still occupied by members of the original family and still a working plantation, is accessible for tours, and only by advance reservation. Historic homes that can be enjoyed from the roadway include Riverlake, a raised Creole cottage with second-floor walls of bousillage built by Isaac Gaillard on a French land grant; gifted author Ernest Gaines was born there. Others include Northbend, Pleasant View, Bonnie Glen, Austerlitz, the complex of historic structures called Maison Chenal, LeBeau House, and along the Mississippi River, the Labatut House.

Across from Parlange, which is one of the finest examples of French colonial architecture in the state, an early plantation outbuilding now houses the Pointe Coupée Parish Museum and visitor information center. This historic cabin on the banks of False River, its dovetailed hand-sawn timbers secured with wooden pegs and insulated with bousillage, was donated to the parish in memory of Allan Ramsey, prominent local landowner whose invention of a sugarcane harvester greatly contributed to the mechanization of agriculture in the area.

A beautiful new bridge, the longest cable-stayed bridge in the country, connects New Roads with the world across the Mississippi River (long accessible only by ferry), but

Pointe Coupée Parish Museum and Tourist Center

life continues to be centered around historic Main Street and False River, a water-oriented lifestyle that's so casual and relaxed that the area now attracts large numbers of weekenders and retirees to enjoy championship fishing, boating, sailing, waterskiing, speedboat racing, and other water sports. Indeed, in 2010 it was named a Playful City USA Community, and the following year New Roads began a Harvest Festival to commemorate the variety of crops still produced in the area. Popular restaurants have decks overlooking the river plus boat docks and lower-story lounges where bathing suits are permissible attire, Music on Main has downtown dancing to live music periodically, and there's a public boat launch right in the middle of town across from the Catholic Church. The Fourth of July boat parade on False River is one of the area's most popular and hilarious events (with water balloons flying), rivaled only by the long-established Mardi Gras parades on dry land. The morning Community Center Carnival parade is Louisiana's oldest outside New Orleans, and it is followed in the afternoon on Fat Tuesday by the Lions Carnival parade, with dozens of floats, marching bands, and thousands of onlookers lining Main Street.

Since 1847 New Roads has been the seat of government for the parish, and the present 1930s Romanesque Revival courthouse would look right at home in the French countryside. In front of the courthouse is a statue of Maj. Gen. John Archer LeJeune, World War I hero who became commandant of the Marine Corps. On the opposite end of the historic downtown district is the monument and tomb of Julien Poydras in front of the former school building

St. Mary's of False River

that is now the National Register-listed Julien Poydras Museum and Art Center, home to the local historical society and tourism offices as well as a center for arts and cultural activities. In between these two anchor buildings, the New Roads Main Street community is a busy, bustling place with antique and gift shops, fine restaurants, a coffeehouse, police station, post office, and overnight accommodations. The present Gothic Revival St. Mary's of False River dates from 1904.

A Main Street community since 2000, New Roads has benefitted from downtown rehab projects that keep the area fresh and vital, with inviting landscaping and restored historic façades on many of the early buildings. One of the busiest commercial spaces is Satterfield's, directly on False River, which began life in 1917 as Satterfield Motors, Pointe Coupée's first permanent automobile dealership; a vintage model Ford along with many historic images and artifacts are still on display. Today the space houses upscale boutique shopping at the Main Street entrance, a corridor of exhibits leading up to the Upper Deck restaurant with immense windows overlooking False River, and a lower-level waterfront Landing Lounge that has live music on weekends as well as ice and gas for boaters.

Also right on False River is Morel's, offering waterfront dining, antiques, and accommodations around a courtyard garden; it began around the turn of the century when a couple of brothers started baking bread and pies, then opened the first inn and restaurant in 1926. On Main Street across from the riverside is the popular MaMama's Restaurant in a wonderful historic building with a second-

Satterfield's

MaMama's Restaurant

story wrought-iron balcony and some of the best food in the state. Both MaMama's and Morel's have been recipients of Main Street rehabilitation incentive grants.

Pointe Coupée's catchy promo slogan is "Where River History & French Culture Collide," and there's no better place to savor this character and atmosphere than right in the historic Main Street community of New Roads, still the heart and soul of town.

Opelousas

Population: 16,634

Promotional slogans for this area call it "Gumbo for your Soul," and that's just what it is, the magical and mysterious amalgam of many parts harmoniously blending diverse ingredients and influences into a delicious and delightful experience. *Le Poste des Opelousas* had its beginnings around 1720 as a military station and trading post where French *coureurs des bois* (woods runners or trappers) had already established trade relations with the small band of resident Native Americans known as the Opelousas, a name roughly translated as "black leg." They were soon joined by other immigrants of many nationalities—French soldiers from other isolated frontier garrisons who had taken Indian wives, Creoles of European ancestry born in this country, Spanish, Anglos, Germans, Italians, Acadian exiles, African slaves bringing all-important agricultural skills, and a large number of *gens de couleur libres*, free people of color, their unique contributions combining, not always painlessly, to make Opelousas a rich gumbo of blended cultures.

In 1764 a large grant of land in the Opelousas area was given to Louis Pellerin, who was appointed commandant of the administrative district by the French colonial governor. By 1769 there were one hundred families living in the town, which had become an important mid-way stopping point for travel between Louisiana's earliest settlements at Natchitoches and New Orleans. There are even a few rare structures dating from this period left in town, like the beautiful French Colonial Michel Prudhomme Home. In 1805 the legislative council of the expansive Territory of Orleans created the County of Opelousas as one of twelve original counties, with provisions for the construction of a courthouse and establishment of a judicial system with judges and justices of the peace.

This was apparently none too soon. A newly arrived Methodist minister wrote from Opelousas in 1806, the year the local Methodist church was founded as the state's

first Protestant church, that the local residents spent the Sabbath "in frolicking and gambling." Commandant Pellerin himself had proved to be even more corrupt, stealing the government-issued resettlement supplies from destitute Acadians, running rival traders out of business, and even commandeering sacred vessels in a feud with the local priest over the rowdy tavern Pellerin operated right next to St. Landry Catholic Church, which had been established in 1774. The Spanish governor of Louisiana noted that Pellerin "sought to steal everything he could" and forced him to retire from public life. At the first meeting of the St. Landry Police Jury, immediate construction of a jail was ordered, to be built adjacent to the debtors' prison. (More than a century later, the long tenure of legendary Sheriff Cat Doucet revived the area's reputation as a haven for gambling and prostitution.)

By the time Imperial-St. Landry Parish was created in 1807, with Opelousas as parish seat of government and the minutes of the police jury kept in both French and English, the surrounding lush prairieland was producing such an abundance of livestock that it was called the cattle kingdom of the United States. Vast herds were driven to the landing on Bayou Courtableau for shipment to New Orleans markets, a treacherous trip that could take weeks across the Atchafalaya Basin and through bayous to the Mississippi River. Besides being the parochial seat of government and justice, the town of Opelousas developed into a busy commercial center supplying the needs of the outlying cattle ranches and cotton or sugarcane plantations, and the arrival of the first steamboats in the 1820s

proved to be a great boon to commerce.

After Baton Rouge fell to Federal forces during the Civil War, Opelousas served briefly as the state capital in 1862, with the handsome Greek Revival home of Lt. Governor Charles Homere Mouton serving as the governor's mansion and the legislature convening in the courthouse and the LaCombe Hotel. After a single legislative session, the Confederate capital of the state moved in 1863 farther north to Shreveport as Union Gen. Nathaniel Banks occupied Opelousas. When a skirmish was fought near Opelousas, wounded soldiers were treated on the front lawn of the Labyche-Estorge Home (ca. 1827) by the resident physician. The turbulent war years were followed by even more trying times during Reconstruction.

The coming of the railroad in the 1880s brought increased connections to the outside world and an accompanying ease in transporting crops and merchandise to market. The railroad also brought out the best of Opelousas—its hospitability in accepting with open arms immigrants and refugees from distant parts. The 1927 Great Mississippi River Flood saw the population of Opelousas double with washed-out refugees, but even earlier, in the spring of 1907, three "Orphan Trains" had arrived in Opelousas, carrying abandoned and orphaned children from the overcrowded New York Foundling Hospital being delivered for placement with Catholic families in the area. Escorted by several Sisters of Charity and a couple of nurses, some two thousand tiny tots, tagged with identification numbers, were sent to various parts of Louisiana; in the Opelousas area, perhaps 175 to 180 children were assigned to prospective parents who took

them into their homes, some for love and some no doubt for the prospect of free labor. A former Union Pacific Freight Depot has been restored to house the Louisiana Orphan Train Museum, complete with documents and artifacts as well as a moving mural by well-known artist Robert Dafford.

The Orphan Train Museum is located in *Le Vieux Village*, established in 1988 by the Opelousas Tourism and Activities Committee and filled with relocated architecturally significant historic structures, including a typical early two-room schoolhouse, the Palmetto African-American Methodist Church, an 1890 doctor's office, a steam locomotive, Emar Andrepont's country store, the 1850 Perkins family home, and even a nineteenth-century outhouse. The Venus House, at one time owned by a free woman of color named Venus and now listed on the National Register of Historic Places, is a superb example of typical Creole architecture dating from the mid- to late-1700s and is considered one of the oldest structures in the area. There's also an exhibit pertaining to Jim Bowie, who lived in the area after the War of 1812, capturing bears and roping alligators on family lands near Bayou Boeuf, floating logs down the bayou from the family sawmill to Opelousas, slave trading with the Lafitte brothers and their band of pirates, and honing his skills with his famous dueling knife before dying at age thirty-seven at the Alamo; an ancient live oak tree in the middle of Opelousas' historic downtown area, over 350 years old and measuring nineteen feet around, is called the Jim Bowie Oak. During the holiday season the Lighting of the

Village features thousands of twinkling lights and holiday music, horse and buggy rides, arts, crafts, and Santa Claus. Tourist information is available here, as well as maps of the walking tour through the Opelousas Historic District downtown.

When the town of Opelousas was formally incorporated by the legislature in 1821, it included all land within one-half mile of the courthouse, which is still the focus of the tree-lined National Historic District and the Main Street community, the wonderful mix of significant commercial, governmental, and residential structures making this a downtown that is very much alive. Brick sidewalks dating from the 1830s pass antebellum, Victorian, and turn-of-the-century homes; the Queen

St. Landry Parish Courthouse

Anne Victorian Veazie-Pavy Home, built of cypress in 1905 at a cost of $5,000, is a spectacular example. The art-deco St. Landry Parish Courthouse is the fifth on its site and dates from 1939; Lawyers' Row across from the courthouse has a group of century-old legal offices. The old Opelousas City Hall was built of handmade brick in 1888 as a Victorian marketplace; the three-story brick Romanesque Revival Old Federal Building dates from 1890; and the neoclassical Union Bank building, dating from around 1910 and now owned by St. Landry Parish, is currently used by the drug court.

The Palace Café, open since 1927, is Opelousas' oldest restaurant. And then there's Shute's Drugstore, ca. 1924, which housed the Old Star Barber Shop where Otis Welch gave a shave in 1932 to a stranger named Clyde Barrow,

**Above: Old Opelousas City Hall
Opposite page: Downtown Opelousas**

who would be pumped full of lead by federal lawmen a few days later in North Louisiana, along with his gun moll Bonnie. In all, the century beginning in 1840 saw the construction of most of the structures that contribute to Opelousas having such an outstanding commercial and governmental sector.

Opelousas' Main Street program, established in 1990, contributes to downtown's viability through its mission to build long-term sustainable revitalization while embracing projects promoting cultural diversity, tourism, and business development as well as beautifying and celebrating the community's history. Through redevelopment incentive grants, the Main Street program has encouraged the rehabbing of historic structures like the 1921 Greco shoe repair shop just across from the courthouse, which now houses the popular Back In Time restaurant and gift shop, as well as sponsoring projects and special events drawing people to the downtown area. Wild About Downtown! created thirty-one art banners designed and decorated by students and artists and Fiddle Mania placed decoratively painted fiberglass fiddles throughout downtown, which are no longer displayed. Music & Market and November's French Friday on Main Street combine indigenous music and foods for fun gatherings, and in conjunction with the Opelousas Historic District Commission, awards are given in recognition of deserving beautification and restoration efforts.

The Opelousas Museum and Interpretive Center houses collections interpreting the diverse influences throughout the period of Opelousas' development, and

the Creole Heritage Folklife Center is committed to nurturing the unique Creole identity. Evangeline Downs Racetrack provides thoroughbred and quarter horse racing excitement and shows why so many winning jockeys in national track events began their careers in this area.

Festivals in Opelousas also commemorate important aspects of the town's heritage and culture. The Louisiana Yambilee Festival was begun in 1946 in this region where sweet potatoes have long been a major cash crop. The Spice and Music Festival is a natural in this Cajun/Creole Food Capital of Louisiana, where internationally famous Louisiana chef Paul Prudhomme learned to cook and the late great Tony Chachere concocted the Creole seasoning that allows cooks all over the world to put a little spice in their lives and on their plates. Tony Chachere products, including his best-selling cookbooks, have been produced in Opelousas since 1972.

The Original Southwest Louisiana Zydeco Festival got its start in 1982 as a means of keeping alive this unique genre in the city officially named the Zydeco Capital of the World. Opelousas is known as the birthplace of this unique music, and it was home of flamboyant King of Zydeco, the late Grammy-winning Clifton Chenier, as famous for his flashing gold tooth and flowing cape and crown as for his music. Opelousas Main Street hosts an annual Zydeco Breakfast in conjunction with its Labor Day celebrations. Like everything else in Opelousas, Zydeco is a blending of diverse ingredients, with Afro-American, Cajun, and Afro-Caribbean antecedents, the result of what Acadian scholar and author Dr. Carl Brasseaux calls "cross-cultural pollination." The name Zydeco evolved from the French phrase *les haricots sont pas sales*, literally meaning *the snap beans are not salty*, a metaphor for tough times when even salt meat for seasoning beans was hard to come by.

Perhaps that's the secret Opelousas learned long ago, the determination to turn tough times into triumphs, making music of misfortunes and making merry while performing the most mundane chores (only a Cajun could turn the hard work of butchering a pig into a day-long party called a *boucherie*). This is an area that nurtures a deep and abiding respect for its history and heritage, celebrating *all* the diverse influences that only serve to add spice to the luscious gumbo of life in Opelousas.

Opposite page: Downtown Opelousas

Plaquemine

Population: 7,119

It has historically been defined by its propitious location, so it is hardly surprising that Plaquemine today retains a deep and abiding sense of place. In its extensive downtown historic district are reminders of every step of the way throughout its unique history, from the river and bayou to the lock and railroad and Louisiana's first interstate roadway, from the party-wall commercial corridor structures to the varied architectural styles of homes built of virgin cypress hauled from the Atchafalaya swamps. And the Main Street program here, along with other dedicated groups, is determined to preserve it all in such a way that downtown remains a vital and much appreciated center of life.

In the early days, waterways were the main means of transportation, and all of the small communities that developed at the confluence of bayou and river waters back then were defined by their sites—none more so than Plaquemine, settled beginning some time before 1775 (tombs in the cemetery have dates as early as 1779) and soon to become an important trade center. It was situated right where the Mississippi River meets Bayou

Plaquemine, an all-important passageway inland from the river for the Acadian exiles, those resilient French farmers and fishermen deported from their homes in Nova Scotia beginning in 1755 and struggling to reunite and rebuild their lives in Louisiana. American poet Henry Wadsworth Longfellow's epic *Evangeline*, the fictionalized version of this tragic *dérangement*, extols the beauties of Bayou Plaquemine, which was named by resident Native Americans for the numerous persimmon trees along its banks. The waterway is mentioned in Iberville's journals as early as 1699 and is shown on a 1732 map rendered by geographer St. d'Anville as *Rre. des Plakemines.*

Bayou Plaquemine was vital to interior settlement and the flow of regional commerce, but it was often impassable due to logjams. Soon after the Civil War, the bayou was completely divorced from the river to help control interior flooding, but the demands of the booming timber and fishing industries necessitated opening a convenient channel between the harvest areas of the Atchafalaya Basin and processing areas along the Mississippi. Bayou Plaquemine became the northern terminus of the Intracoastal Canal system after a lock was erected to control bayou water levels, ease movement of boat traffic from one water level to the other, and provide a shortcut from the river into the state's interior heartland.

Finally completed in 1909 after a fourteen-year struggle with unstable soil, yellow fever epidemics, and contractor bankruptcies, the Plaquemine Lock, with its unique gravity-flow design, was the highest freshwater lift lock in the world; it would later be modernized with hydraulic

Plaquemine Lockhouse

pumps and steam power. Passage through it shortened the route to the Gulf through Atchafalaya waterways by more than one hundred miles. Col. George W. Goethals, later chief engineer for the Panama Canal, was the designer for the inner workings of the Plaquemine Lock, which was also noted for the Dutch-style architecture of the lockhouse with its unusual stepped parapet gables.

Now preserved as a State Historic Site, the Plaquemine Lock serves as the focal point of a bustling downtown area, but this did not happen without another struggle, for the state had designs on the area as part of an expanded highway project. Only the desperate efforts of local publisher Gary Hebert and other preservationists kept this significant structure from being demolished and the bayou filled in. Today from its hilltop location and safely listed on the National Register of Historic Places, which

provides a modicum of protection from misguided efforts at progress, the little Dutch lockhouse—a symbol of the hope that yes, preservation and progress can sometimes move forward hand in hand without trampling each other—overlooks the award-winning Bayou Plaquemine Waterfront Park. The park features inviting pier walkways along the bayou, covered pavilions and picnic areas, scenic overlooks, boat docks and floating piers for fishing. The park also contains the recently renovated Nadler's Foundry and Machine Shop, considered to have been the south's last foundry, family owned and operated for 150 years; the original office building has been turned into meeting space, and the foundry into a ten thousand-square-foot open-air pavilion. There are hopes of purchasing additional property.

The first steamboat to enter the lock was the Carrie B. Schwing, used by the local Schwing Lumber and Shingle Company to tow prehistoric cypress lumber. Miss Carrie herself christened the lock in April 1909 by breaking a bottle of champagne against its wall. Iberville Parish, which Plaquemine serves as seat of government, was the center of South Louisiana's cypress timber industry for half a century beginning in the 1870s, with nine lumber mills along Bayou Plaquemine employing thousands of people, the sawmills producing over 1.5 million board feet during peak years. The lasting legacy of this prosperous lumber industry is the large number of architectural gems scattered throughout the tree-shaded National Register-listed Historic District that stretches from the river and Hwy. 1 to the railroad tracks. Residences range in style

from stately Greek Revival to exuberantly colorful Queen Anne, Colonial, shotguns and bungalows; along Eden, Main, and Railroad Avenue, some commercial buildings share common walls and massive governmental structures are mostly Italianate or Beaux Arts architectural style.

This outstanding district, accepted in 1989 by the U.S. Department of Interior—National Trust for Historic Preservation, contains some 120 structures of architectural significance dating from the 1840s through the 1930s. At one time there were many more, but Plaquemine is situated on a sharp bend in the Mississippi River, and cave-ins over

Above: Colorful example of Queen Anne architecture Opposite page: Bayou Plaquemine Waterfront Park

the years, especially in 1888, sadly plunged a number of homes and businesses—even whole streets—into the waters.

A fine example of Greek Revival downtown is the columned structure built in 1848 as the parish courthouse and later used as city hall, its plans drawn by famed New Orleans architect James Gallier. Located just across from the Plaquemine Lock State Historic Site, the old government building is now the Iberville Museum, its operations overseen by Plaquemine Main Street and a museum board, one of three courthouses still in use (there are also two historic former Plaquemine High Schools, one ca. 1911 and one ca. 1931, which have been repurposed). It is full of interesting permanent and visiting exhibits and artifacts, including the original 1835 incorporation papers of the city of Plaquemine, an old horse-drawn buggy called a *Jumper* because it bounced across cane fields on its four-foot-tall wheels, a Model T, and a twenty-four-foot cypress *bateau* with a Nadler putt-putt two-cycle engine made in Plaquemine. Courthouse operations moved in 1906 to a three-story Beaux Arts building called "The Great Temple of Justice," with double columns supporting a portico, located on Railroad Ave. and now used as the city hall. Another magnificent Greek Revival structure downtown is the two and one-half-story brick and frame St. Basil's Academy, now a private home but built in the 1850s as a Catholic school and home of the Sisters Marianites of the Holy Cross.

The Church of the Holy Communion was built in 1913 in the picturesque Gothic Revival style beloved by

Above: Iberville Museum
Opposite page: St. Basil's Academy

Episcopalians, and nowhere is there a finer example of Italian Romanesque Revival architecture than St. John the Evangelist Church, dominating the downtown streetscape, a massive 1920s structure with heavy round columns and enormous oak doors, campanile, archways, and an open-truss interior ceiling towering above the impressive balastrino altar of marble.

The Plaquemine Depot Antique Market is located in the old Union Pacific Railroad Depot, built in 1928 and the center of downtown activity when the railroads were running full steam; Plaquemine was a thriving center of commerce with hotels, restaurants, and retail businesses, and the railroad ran right through the heart of town. Today trains still rumble past the depot; the Union Pacific

Railroad calls this its second busiest railway in the nation. In the old depot, cultural activities and events have been highlighting local heritage since the building was reclaimed by Plaquemine Main Street as part of its downtown revitalization program, and in its 1998 reincarnation as the Depot Market, the building has been filled with American and European antiques, decorative items, jewelry, baby clothes, and artwork. Another building reclaimed and adapted for new usage is the Neo-Classical Plaquemine High School, now available as a venue for recreational activities and other events.

The downtown historic district sits on a 358-acre Spanish land grant made to Antoine Rodriguez in 1782. Plaquemine's Main Street District is within the National Register Historic District of twenty-one blocks and has been established since 1992, designed to restore the downtown area as a viable marketplace and center of community activity through façade grants to rehabilitate public and private buildings that contribute to the community fabric. The Main Street program here also sponsors other initiatives like installing attractive ornamental lighting and street banners as well as brick sidewalk pavers along Railroad Avenue and organizing downtown business owners for cooperative group projects and informational programs. The renovation of the old depot to house small businesses and as a site for seasonal activities has been one of Main Street's most significant contributions.

With funding assistance from the city, corporate-financed events, and grants, Main Street also sponsors and assists with annual events to showcase the downtown district and generate revenue, such as the July Fourth Festival, the Main Street Festival of Christmas Lights, and the St. Jude Car, Truck, and Motorcycle Show at Bayou Plaquemine Waterfront Park. For more than half a century, downtown Plaquemine has also been the location for the annual Cub Scout Soapbox Derby Car Race, with a parade, beauty pageants, and dozens of homemade cars piloted by young Scouts from across South Louisiana and southwest Mississippi whizzing down the Mississippi River levee onto Main Street between the Plaquemine Lock and the Iberville Museum.

Plaquemine Main Street sees its mission as maintaining a vibrant downtown where people live, work, and play. This mission is interpreted as "an on-going program that is essentially the management of change over time," a sensible view of accepting the inevitability of change while recognizing the necessity of directing that change so that it preserves historic buildings while producing not just short-term improvements in appearance but long-term commitments toward economic and cultural growth. Main Street works to strengthen and enhance business and resident relationships with local and state government while promoting job creation and retention, critical to revitalization success.

The Plaquemine area is part of the Atchafalaya National Heritage Area, the Louisiana Scenic Bayou ByWays program, and is on the Greater River Road Scenic Byways within the Mississippi Basin. Surrounding the town of Plaquemine are magnificent antebellum plantations amidst extensive sugarcane fields (some, like the vast agricultural lands of A. Wilbert's & Sons, have been turned into championship golf courses like The Island, on Louisiana's Audubon Golf Trail), interspersed with modern petro-chemical companies like Dow Chemical, the largest in the state, that rely on the river for transportation. In town, there are other recognized districts of interest, including the local Historic District, the verdant Garden District, and Old Turnerville along the river. But the heart and soul of Plaquemine today, as in the old days, remains the downtown National Register Historic District and, within it, the lively and lovely Main Street community, looking to the future while maintaining its well-grounded and distinctive sense of place.

Ponchatoula

Population: 6,559

Louisiana's Main Streets are fondly described as "like Mayberry, only the diner sells gumbo and Aunt Bea does a wicked two-step." But here in Ponchatoula, L'il Opie would be out in the fields picking berries with the other kids instead of whistling his way to the ol' fishing hole, and Aunt Bea would be sneaking a sip of strawberry wine! This is strawberry country, dubbed the Strawberry Capital of the World, and the Ponchatoula Strawberry Festival for decades has been one of the state's largest and best festivals, a fundraiser for non-profit and charitable organizations that attracts thousands to one of the state's loveliest little downtown Main Streets.

You'd never know it now to view this vibrant and bustling downtown area with its well-kept turn-of-the-century storefronts, popular antiques shops, and upstairs living quarters, but a 1980s highway expansion that lasted for a miserable four years cut beautiful trees that had shaded the area for decades and put *out* of business most of the businesses along Pine Street, as Hwy. 22 is called through downtown, the focal point of Ponchatoula's Main

Street Historic District. Of the dozens of viable businesses at the start of the construction project to widen the roadway from two to four lanes—a busy assortment of hardware stores, barber shops, groceries, dime stores, and the like—only three were still in business when the project was completed.

But just like the area's persistent strawberry farmers who learned to persevere through hardships like late freezes and long droughts that sometimes ruined an entire year's crop, Ponchatoula's downtown property owners and business people were equally determined to survive, and survive they did. In 1989 the Chamber of Commerce came up with the idea of proclaiming Ponchatoula "America's

Antique City," and city officials, the Tangipahoa Parish Convention and Visitors Bureau, local businesses, and property owners joined together to support the idea. Downtown property owners assessed themselves 1 percent of sales or one month's rent, merchants were assessed their share, and the monies raised were designated for advertising and development; within a year, downtown occupancy rates rose 80 percent. In 1991 Ponchatoula became part of Louisiana's Main Street program, with a manager positively brilliant at thinking outside the box.

In preparation for the birth of "America's Antique City," the largest problem facing the founders was the condition of the vacant buildings. Every single building needed painting. An eighteen-wheeler loaded with Pratt Lambert paint was donated, and a busload of prison inmates painted a grand total of sixty-three buildings under the supervision of the Louisiana State Division of Historic Preservation. The newly spruced-up structures were quickly occupied, and the revitalization of downtown Ponchatoula became a success story brought about by a true group effort, a combination of determination and hard work by the state, the city, property owners, and volunteers.

Since then, Main Street, in conjunction with the state Division of Historic Preservation, has continued to help with rehab incentive matching grants and tax advantages for restoring some of the picturesque downtown structures along Pine and Railroad Avenue, a number of which date from the early 1900s and are brick with gabled or shaped parapets, arched fenestration, decorative brick courses, cast-iron posts and ornamentation, and cornice trim.

Paul's Café

Many of the two-story structures have balconies and upper-level occupancy, either offices or loft living spaces that keep the downtown area active twenty-four hours a day. Today the Main Street community, a National Register Historic District three blocks long that includes sixty-seven buildings, has a high occupancy rate. This is a vibrant and active downtown area, full of restaurants and cafes, bars and banks, feed stores, attorney and realty offices, and many antiques shops, with a constant flow of tourist traffic as well as resident business. Main Street façade grants have assisted with the innovative restorations of historic commercial structures like the Pflanze Hotel Building, the Masonic Temple building housing Lockheed Martin and a realty company downstairs with apartments upstairs, and the Campbell Building headquarters of JaniKing. Paul's Café, in a large brick former drugstore building with molded cornice and corner entry, has an

apartment upstairs and fine home cooking downstairs. Tile-roofed St. Joseph's Catholic Church is the oldest church in Ponchatoula, begun in 1866, with the present impressive brick structure erected in 1927. All Saints Episcopal was begun in 1873, its first building lost in a tornado. The tiny Collinswood School Museum occupies a former one-room schoolhouse now filled with local artifacts, and the local weekly newspaper, *The Ponchatoula Times*, has its headquarters downtown as well.

One of the paper's most popular columnists is Ole Hardhide, described as living "in the center of Ponchatoula in his own gated condo, with pool. . . . He writes about Ponchatoula goings-on that could get an editor in trouble—even in this mellow, unique, sub-tropical small Louisiana city." And indeed, this beloved city mascot, actually a live alligator who not only writes a gossipy newspaper column

Above and opposite page: Downtown Ponchatoula

**Above: Collingswood School Museum
Opposite page: Ponchatoula Country Market**

but also has his own bank account, luxuriates at the entrance to the popular Country Market in the historic train depot, erected in 1854 and rebuilt after it was burned in the Civil War. The present structure was built in the mid-1890s and has been restored to house a co-op market for all manner of arts and handcrafts, jewelry, clothing, jellies, and sweets.

Besides Ole Hardhide's "condo, with pool," the depot is flanked by a Mail Car art gallery/museum and a 1912 steam locomotive used to haul huge red cypress logs from the forested swamps south of town when Ponchatoula was a booming lumber town. The timber industry and several huge sawmills that opened in the 1920s attracted so many new residents that town businesses boomed; where other small towns rolled up the sidewalks at dark, it was said you could get a haircut in downtown Ponchatoula on a Saturday night all the way to midnight. Not until 1956 was the last stand of virgin tidewater red cypress harvested.

The locomotive and the huge cypress log at Ponchatoula Country Market are remnants of the town's origins back in the mid-1800s when the New Orleans, Jackson & Great Northern Railroad, later the Illinois Central, put Ponchatoula on the map. James B. Clark, surveyor and engineer for the railroad, envisioned a community in the midst of the thick piney woods on the first dry land north of the swamps. Joining forces with one of the area's earliest settlers and largest landowners, William Akers, in 1854 Clark laid out the town in a grid pattern with streets one hundred feet wide—numbered streets running parallel to the railroad tracks and streets named for trees running horizontally. Clark reserved a central square for railroad company use and designated space for other public squares in each quarter of the town. The name Ponchatoula came from a Choctaw Indian word meaning "hanging hair," apparently for the prolific Spanish moss.

Even before it was incorporated in 1861, Ponchatoula had attracted settlers, and the village soon had livery stables, small wooden stores, and a few hotels. The coming of the railroad changed the face of the area from sparsely settled piney woods and cypress swamps to a series of little towns and sawmills, with rising land values, farms cultivating truck crops, and small businesses to support these endeavors. Then the Civil War came, and the

railroad line drew repeated raids by Federal troops, who ransacked Ponchatoula and destroyed the train depot and area bridges. The village of Ponchatoula, in the economic disaster that ensued, had a post-war population in 1870 of 320 people.

But in 1896 the *Hammond Graphic* ran an article extolling the virtues of Ponchatoula, its tree-shaded streets lined with new dwellings and businesses, the rich fields producing boundless truck crops, all in all a fine setting offering opportunities "for parties who possess a reasonable amount of pluck and energy, except for lawyers, of which we have none and do not need. Also physicians, we have the healthiest country on the globe," forcing the two local doctors to farm and run the local hotel due to the dearth of paying patients.

Not until the opening years of the twentieth century did Ponchatoula and surrounding Tangipahoa Parish see the advent of a prosperous strawberry industry, made possible by the development of reliable refrigerated rail cars allowing the marketing and distribution of perishable products to much wider areas. Before refrigeration, Louisiana berries often melted in the heat during shipment; one faraway customer wired, "Car arrived, also the crates. What did you do with the berries?" after the ice had melted enroute and the berries turned to juice before arrival. New and hardier varieties of berries were developed to hold up better when transported long distances, and farmers' associations and organizations assisted local growers with marketing and quality control. As the local farmers prospered, the downtown area grew,

filling with fine brick buildings occupied by businesses and support services for the farm operations.

Peak years for strawberry production were the 1930s; in 1931, 197 railcars of berries were shipped from Ponchatoula in a single day, each carload holding 736 crates and each crate holding twenty-four pints of berries, so that it took four express trains to pull the load. The total for the 1931 season was close to eighty-five million pints of berries, valued at some $9 million (unfortunately the following year would be a disastrous one of heavy rain and hail storms). But even in the early 1900s whole trainloads of berries were being shipped to Chicago and other distant markets.

"Of course everybody in Ponchatoula knows that we have the most ideal climate, soil, water . . . and that our strawberries bring the highest prices," said the *Ponchatoula Enterprise* in 1921. As harvest season neared, the town bustled with produce buyers and migrant workers; boarding houses and hotels filled and businesses boomed. Farmers lined the streets along the railroad tracks in horse-drawn wagons and later in trucks, waiting to load crates of berries into railroad cars. Local schools accommodated their schedules to strawberry season, so that even the children were able to help with berry picking, label pasting, and crate packing; in the farm families, every member of the household pitched in, their labor augmented by thousands of migrant workers and even passing hoboes, called "wandering Willies" and dusty drifters.

In 1930 local entrepreneur Marion T. Fannaly shipped 500,000 pounds of berries on the Illinois Central to St. Louis and Chicago; it was Fannaly who began processing late berries for ice cream and confectionary manufacturers, built his own refrigeration plant to produce ice and provide cold storage, had a veneer mill to make berry boxes, and established a number of other businesses. With little formal education, Fannaly went from selling peanuts on Ponchatoula street corners as a child to owning the world's largest strawberry and shrimp freezing enterprises. The site of his freezing plant is now home to the iconic Elmer Candy Company, producers of Gold Brick Easter eggs and other famed delicacies.

The Ponchatoula Strawberry Festival, touted as the second largest festival in the state behind Mardi Gras, is always a top contender for *Country Roads Magazine*'s Favorite Festival; for over four decades it has drawn enormous crowds for live music, culinary cook-offs, golf and bass tournaments, beauty pageants, and tons of fun. Other special events, such as the St. Patrick's Day parade (cabbages and potatoes are the throws of choice for St. Paddy's), draw crowds to enjoy downtown Ponchatoula's historic district and honor its heritage. The Christmas holiday season is kicked off by Downtown Lighting the first Friday in December. Other events include a BBQ cook-off called Party in the Pits, spring and fall Antique Trade Days the first full weekends of March and November, and a Labor Day Getaway. The BerryPatch Quilt and Art Expo is held every other year in October, and Ponchatoula now participates in the new five-parish Louisiana Northshore Quilt Trail, established to showcase the beauty of quiltmaking by exhibiting artistic interpretations of quilt blocks while promoting community cooperation and encouraging tourism; maps allow viewing of colorful quilt blocks creatively installed on the outside of homes, barns, buildings, and businesses. Ponchatoula's very popular Christmas in July citywide sale takes place mid-summer in America's Antique City with *only* 150 or so shopping days 'til Christmas.

There's even an Easter Bonnet Stroll; look carefully, and you just might spot Aunt Bea. Unless she's stepped into one of the local watering holes to have a little nip of strawberry wine while L'il Opie goes tubing down the Tangipahoa River.

Ruston

Population: 21,859

A heavily trafficked cross-country interstate highway running through its northern edge has helped this college town grow into one of the largest of Louisiana's Main Street communities, but Ruston's eighteen-block downtown historic district has managed to retain the traditional charm and vitality of its early years. This is thanks to a concerned citizenry and sensible municipal administrations that, even before Ruston became a Main Street community in 1989, actively pursued downtown revitalization with some innovative programs of their own.

The seat of government for Lincoln Parish, Ruston was founded shortly after the Civil War when the Vicksburg, Shreveport, and Pacific Railroad strung its tracks across North Louisiana. In 1873 land was purchased in the area by Robert Edwin Russ, a planter and civic leader who would serve as Lincoln Parish sheriff in the late 1870s. The well-travelled Mr. Russ had been born in Florida, attended school in Tennessee, and migrated to Alabama, Mississippi, and then Louisiana, where in 1855 he married and later had thirteen children.

Russ donated 640 acres to form a town around the train depot, which would eventually be called Russ Town or Ruston. Lots for homes and businesses were laid out by former Union Army surveyors and sold beginning in 1883 for $375 each. The early commercial development hugged the railroad line; before the town was established, merchants and shopkeepers from neighboring communities had hawked food and supplies to the railroad workers from tents lining the track. Ruston was incorporated in 1884 as the seat of justice and government in a parish named during Reconstruction for President Abraham Lincoln.

When a second railroad, this one running north-south, came to town in 1900, the area expanded even more, the

downtown commercial corridor filling with fine brick structures housing supply merchants and service providers for the surrounding cotton farmers as well as students and faculty at the growing institutes of higher learning in the area, one right in town and several others in the vicinity. Town founder Robert E. Russ was a trustee of Ruston College, which in 1894 would become the Industrial Institute and College of Louisiana, now Louisiana Tech University. The GI Bill enabled many World War II vets to continue their educations here, and today the three local universities (Louisiana Tech, Grambling, and UL Monroe) have a combined enrollment of some twenty-four thousand students. Additional students who are visually challenged come to Ruston's nationally recognized Louisiana Center for the Blind to learn the skills necessary for independent living and employability.

The train still runs through Ruston, and what a thrill it is to see the powerful engines speeding through the big

Historic Ruston. *Louis Fuller Marbury, used with permission of Becky Napper.*

archway toward the beautiful downtown Railroad Park along the tracks. But it is even more gratifying to see the downtown revitalization that was six years in the planning and is being implemented in stages, making a dramatic transformation with a combination of federal, state, and local funding and support.

Decades-old, unsightly above-ground powerlines are being replaced with underground utilities, and smooth brick-paver sidewalks and easy curbs have made this a bicyclist- and pedestrian-friendly area. Inviting benches, street light standards hung with flower baskets, plentiful parking, and colorful landscaping enhance the appeal and draw patrons to the shops, restaurants, and offices filling downtown's beautifully restored historic buildings.

The eighteen-block downtown historic district is today called "a glimmering gem of history and culture, the true heart of the city." Under the progressive but preservation-minded city administration in 1984, Ruston established a low-interest loan pool with the cooperation of five area banks, working together to provide funding for local businesses, in increments of $10,000, to be used for property improvements. By early 1990, several dozen businesses had undertaken renovations with loaned monies. A strong merchants' association had been established, and it was soon joined by a historic district commission. The Main Street manager, beginning in 1989, has continuously played a strong role in organizing and promoting the downtown area and educating its property owners and businesses about matching façade grants and available tax advantages.

Downtown Ruston is a National Register Historic District, with a number of buildings individually listed. One of those is the Dixie Center for the Arts, the cultural and entertainment highlight of the city. It was built in

Above: Downtown Ruston
Opposite page: Dixie Center for the Arts

1928 as a theater called the Astor, hosting concerts and silent movies for tickets prices ranging from ten to fifty cents. An exquisite crystal chandelier was added to the decor in 1932 when the theater was renamed the Rialto. The '30s brought the tribulations of the Depression and a disastrous fire, but the theater survived to become the Dixie when a 1950s sale to the Dixie Theater Corporation of New Orleans brought improvements like air conditioning and the famous flashing star crowning the marquee. By the mid-1990s the theater had closed its doors for performances and was used only as office space, but the determined citizens of Ruston had other ideas. A decade of fundraisers later, the Dixie was gloriously restored and in 2006 re-opened as a 550-seat community cultural center hosting a full season of concerts and performing arts shows, an artists' gallery, and a venue for events or meetings. The Piney Hills Gallery in the lobby of the Dixie Center for the Arts exhibits the works of some of the many talented artists in the area.

Another downtown restoration that had great impact and served to preserve an important emblem of Ruston's early history was the 2010 Harris Hotel project. Ruston's last remaining railroad hotel, this 1914 Italian Renaissance structure originally featured a heavy, columned balcony and third-floor balustrade, which had been lost over the years due to water damage and deterioration. The local developer who owned the hotel received a Main Street exterior façade grant, supplemented by his own sizable private investment, to replace the front porch and balustrade, as well as to construct a new roof over the balcony to increase

Above: Downtown Ruston
Opposite page: Downtown Ruston with landscaped parking

square footage and to protect the structural longevity of the porch. The Harris Hotel, now rehabilitated, serves as commercial and rental property. Other downtown property owners have redone not only their own business locations but other historic properties as well, assisting with downtown's dramatic transformation.

Today there are banks and fabric and frame shops, jewelers, a nice variety of restaurants and boutiques, pharmacies and attorney's offices, antiques and specialty shops, artists' studios, and an assortment of small and large businesses that keep this downtown area bustling with patrons. Special events and the seasonal downtown Ruston Farmers' Market bring even more crowds to enjoy the ambience. Sponsored in conjunction with the city and local Chamber of Commerce, Main Street events include

Main to Main, a downtown Christmas Open House, Winter Fest, the Cajun Crawl Festival, and Downtown Howl-oween, but the iconic festival here is Ruston's Squire Creek Louisiana Peach Festival in June. In this area long noted for its productive orchards, the Peach Festival was begun in 1950. It traditionally features more than two hundred artisans and vendors at Railroad Marketplace and the Ruston Civic Center, an arts and crafts show, an antique car show, a parade, a rodeo and runs, a pet show, a downtown food court, a fine arts show, and plenty of great music in Railroad Park, not to mention bushels and bushels of those luscious juicy Ruston peaches.

The city of Ruston is home to several museums, including the Lincoln Parish Museum, housed in the 1885 Kidd-Davis home, and the North Louisiana Military Museum (part of the state museum system), which showcases two hundred years of military history. Both museums are within a few minutes' walk of the downtown shopping area. Outdoors enthusiasts will find great fishing and boating on three state park lakes nearby: 6,400-acre Lake Claiborne, 15,000-acre Lake D'Arbonne, and 5,250-acre Caney Lake. The Lincoln Parish Park is famous for its challenging mountain bike trails plus camping, picnicking, hiking, and a thirty-acre lake for boating and swimming. The college athletic events at Louisiana Tech and Grambling always draw big crowds, and there are also many cultural events on the campuses.

Local promoters call Ruston "not just a city, but a community" and "a peach of a place." The Main Street program here sponsors programs and events that leverage that feeling of community, continuing Ruston's longtime commitment to the idea that preservation and progress must march hand in hand into a future firmly rooted in the past but with plenty of energetic economic viability today and tomorrow.

St. Francisville

Population: 1,765

St. Francisville's location, high atop blufflands overlooking the Mississippi River in West Feliciana Parish, has been both its blessing and, by some accounts, its curse. Safe from the floodwaters that obliterated its sister city of Bayou Sara right on the river's banks, St. Francisville was precariously perched on a narrow finger ridge that limited its growth potential, since the town lots fell off steeply into deep hollows on either side of the single main thoroughfare. In a way, this was a good thing, preventing overdevelopment and limiting modern incursions in a historic district where the cozy mix of residential and commercial structures from the nineteenth and early twentieth centuries happily coexist to provide present-day viability. And they can still call it the town that's two miles long and two yards wide, with little exaggeration.

Founded in the opening years of the nineteenth century by predominantly Anglo settlers, the town was an important social, commercial, and cultural center for the extensive cotton plantations surrounding it. Its early streets were rude dirt tracks that herds of cattle and

mule-drawn wagons piled high with crops traveled before descending the steep hill to the port at Bayou Sara for shipment on riverboats to New Orleans and thence the world.

But improvements were soon effected. By 1809 a hotel had been erected, serving as legislative headquarters for the fledgling government of the independent Republic of West Florida when, in 1810, the Anglo settlers joined together to overthrow a weak and corrupt Spanish regime still holding on to the Florida Parishes after the 1803 Louisiana Purchase. Over St. Francisville have flown the flags of more governments than most other parts of the state—France, England, Spain, the West Florida Republic, the State of Louisiana, the Confederacy, and the United States—some of them more than once.

There the Louisiana Territory's third newspaper was established, the state's second library was begun in 1812, a Masonic Lodge was chartered in 1817, and in 1819 an open-air brick market hall was built with arches through which produce wagons could be driven (this would later serve as the town hall). By 1828 the state's first Episcopal congregation outside New Orleans had formed Grace Church.

Right in town there were gristmills and cotton gins, livery stables and haberdasheries, drygoods emporiums, and supply merchants capable of providing everything the plantations needed, from buggies and fine furnishings to coffins and farm tools, often supplying it all on credit against the next year's crop. In 1853 the *St. Francisville Chronicle* reported that, according to the tax rolls, the parish of West Feliciana, with St. Francisville at its core, contained 2,231 free whites, 70 free blacks, and 10,298 slaves producing 2,873 hogheads of sugar, 4,318 barrels of molasses, 334,000 bushels of corn, and 23,860 bales of cotton selling at approximately $70 a bale.

The prosperity of the antebellum Cotton Kingdom gave way after the Civil War to some lean years as the area struggled with a declining economy no longer supported by agriculture. Many of St. Francisville's historic structures fell into disrepair; many of the merchants of the town, some of them Jewish immigrants who had provided the practicalities and financing for the plantation economy, moved to urban areas where the prospects for success seemed more promising. The little town remained,

Opposite page: Grace Church

however, the parish seat of government and commerce, and by the 1970s a movement began, spearheaded by the West Feliciana Historical Society, to foster a renewed appreciation of its history and heritage. An annual Audubon Pilgrimage tour of historic homes encouraged the entire community to work together to spruce up and share its treasures with visitors, and a late 1970s survey documented over 140 downtown buildings of sufficient architectural significance to be listed in 1980 on the National Register of Historic Places in an official Historic District that was expanded in 1982. Many of these historic downtown structures were listed individually on the National Register as well.

When the St. Francisville Main Street program was established in 1994, it was able to provide incentive grants for a great deal of refurbishing and refreshing of

the downtown area, where the practical combination of business and residential use ensures continued vitality. There may still be only a few thousand residents in St. Francisville, but this little Mississippi River town has something many small towns across the country lack: a vital downtown that is very much alive. When the shops close for the evening, the oak-shaded brick sidewalks come alive with dog-walkers and skateboarders and strollers chatting over picket fences with porch-rockers and swing-sitters decompressing on gingerbread-trimmed galleries, before heading down to the local café for food and fellowship as exuberant youngsters carouse and dance to the live local band.

The admittedly slow pace allows for plenty of time to stop and smell the climbing roses and ancient camellias blooming in every yard, and residents wouldn't have it any other way. When a new Mississippi River bridge was first proposed to connect St. Francisville on the east bank of the river with New Roads on the west, replacing the increasingly unreliable state-run car ferry, economic development proponents wanted the raised bridge approaches to go right through the center of the historic district. Determined (some called them "stubborn") townsfolk banded together to push the country's longest cable-stayed bridge farther south, thus saving fragile downtown structures and a quiet way of life from the stress of constant heavy traffic, harmful vibrations, and noise pollution.

While some of the town's historic structures had been fortunate enough to benefit from privately funded facelifts over the years, even more benefitted once St. Francisville

1905 bank building

and picturesque year-round tourist destination. Writing in "Preservation in Print," Linda Rascoe of the Louisiana Main Street Program called St. Francisville's downtown historic district a visual feast, saying "the closely packed, village-like streetscape contributes to the picturesque pastoral setting where the purity and integrity of the architecture provide a tangible sense of history and a major draw for its primary industry, tourism."

The surrounding countryside has dozens of National Register-listed antebellum plantations and glorious nineteenth-century gardens. Rosedown and Oakley Plantations are state historic sites. Four other historic plantations—The Cottage, The Myrtles, Butler Greenwood, and Greenwood—are also open for daily

became an official Main Street community, backed by grants and funding from both state and national Main Street programs designed to breathe new life into the nation's deteriorating downtowns. The grants made to spruce up downtown commercial structures were matched by more than one million dollars in private investments.

From the grandly baroque 1905 bank building housing a nationally popular button jewelry company to the two-story double-galleried 1817 Masonic Lodge and the 1819 Market Hall, and from the simple nineteenth-century structure used to store coffins to the tiny headquarters of the black benevolent/burial society founded in 1883, dozens of downtown buildings benefitted from these grants, turning the entire historic district into a popular

Old Benevolent Society

Wolf-Schlesinger House

center, sharing space with the parish Tourist Commission and Main Street offices.

The enthusiastic Main Street directors in St. Francisville, following the program philosophy of "Promotion, Organization, Economic Revitalization and Design coupled with Preservation," have led the way in spearheading the movement to ensure that the downtown area retains its appeal, with great financial support from the town's Economic Development Fund providing extras like public restrooms, bricked sidewalks, and tourist information kiosks in central locations.

Local festivals are carefully planned to complement the town's history and heritage, bearing in mind the shift in tourism demographics toward more active ecotourism and

tours. There are unsurpassed recreational opportunities in the rugged Tunica Hills. In downtown St. Francisville there are historic churches, bed and breakfasts, a bustling courthouse complex in daily use, plus an oak-shaded public park complete with bandstand that hosts a number of celebrations throughout the year—all on just two major streets. Ongoing restorations of the historic synagogue and first public school, on a site overlooking the Mississippi River, pay tribute to early Jewish contributions to the town, and indeed the wonderful brick Julius Freyhan School was one of the first recipients of a small façade grant the year St. Francisville was designated a Main Street Community. In a restored vintage hardware store, the historical society maintains a fascinating museum and tourist information

Julius Freyhan School

hands-on living history. Many of the smaller festivals—the monthly community arts market in the park, the White Linen Night, the Trick-or-Treat Down Main Street—are designed specifically to draw visitors to the downtown area to shop. The spring pilgrimage showcases area plantation homes and historic townhouses in a fun community frolic as the azaleas are at their peak, while the Audubon Country Birdfest and summer Hummingbird Festival are ideally suited for this area where artist John James Audubon painted dozens of his Birds of America studies in 1821. In June, The Day The War Stopped is a Civil War re-enactment like no other, commemorating not a booming battle but a brief moment of civility in the midst of a bloody struggle when Confederate and Union Masons joined peaceably in the burial of a Yankee gunboat commander in the Episcopal church cemetery downtown. Fall's Garden Symposium and the Yellow Leaf Arts Festival highlight the glorious nineteenth-century gardens of the area and the generations of fine artists who have drawn inspiration from its scenic vistas and bountiful wildlife, while Christmas in the Country draws thousands downtown for a holiday parade, seasonal entertainment, great shopping, and spectacular decorations that transform the entire town into a veritable winter wonderland.

The five members of the St. Francisville Historic District Commission, supported wholeheartedly by an enthusiastic longtime mayor, oversee Main Street activities and preservation projects, with the Main Street director coordinating and combining efforts like co-op advertising and the publication of tour maps and guides. The goal is to promote tourism and encourage the development of new businesses in town while providing the means to preserve its historic character and charm and support existing merchants. It's never easy to find just the right balance between economic development and historic preservation, but St. Francisville seems to be doing just that.

St. Martinville

Population: 6,114

They call it the Cradle of *Cadien* Culture in Louisiana—St. Martinville, birthplace of Acadiana. And so it was. The first exiles driven from Canadian *L'Acadie* by the British arrived here in 1765, 193 struggling souls sent to establish a village and tend cattle on the early *vacherie* of Jean-Antoine Bernard Dauterive. Sent into the Attakapas District, named for the resident Native Americans whose rumored cannibalistic reputation led to the region being regarded "with horror" by most pioneers, the Acadian exiles were minimally provisioned with flour, hardtack, rice, salt pork, beef, tools to clear the land, and seed rice and corn.

These independent souls soon spread out along Bayou Teche and petitioned for land grants of their own, but life was centered around the church built on property provided by Dauterive. Father Jean Louis Civrey, the curate who had accompanied the Acadians, called this new home *"la Nouvelle Acadie"* and his new parish *"L'Eglise des Attakapas."* The church—the mother church of the Acadians—was named for St. Martin de Tours, fourth-century French bishop and patron

St. Martin de Tours Church

saint of horses and soldiers. The present church, a magnificent structure, dates from 1844.

By 1814 the church's parish council had initiated unique lease-purchase agreements with commission merchants and tradesmen, who soon filled charming double-galleried commercial structures like those circling the extensive church square today, preserved in St. Martinville's National Register-listed historic district. When St. Martinville was incorporated in 1817, the local newspaper described it as the most important town in the Attakapas country, with an academy, a number of local trade shops, four attorneys, and several physicians.

Besides thriving commercially as a trade center along the Teche, St. Martinville became a cultural center as well, wistfully nicknamed *Le Petit Paris*, scene of French theatrical performances, operas, and other sophisticated entertainments. Good hotels and regular steamboat service encouraged early Victorian vacationers to partake of the cultural offerings, making the city a fashionable resort for prominent Creole families from the entire region. The 1830s Duchamp Opera House on the square still houses a local theater company upstairs, and the Old Castillo Hotel, a beautiful bayouside inn still accommodating overnight guests, also dates from the 1830s and was said to have been a center for elegant French Royalist entertainments.

The earliest Acadian settlers had certainly been joined over the years by immigrants from many parts, including, no doubt, some aristocratic title-holders escaping the French Revolution. Colorful early twentieth-century Louisiana writer Harnett Kane, always enamoured of a good story,

Duchamp Opera House

refugees from revolutionary France and the slave revolution in Saint-Domingue, "driven by desperation to a part of the globe regarded by their contemporaries in much the same way that twenty-first-century Americans view the backwaters of the Amazon basin."

And yet there still remains Duchamp Opera House & Mercantile, and the *Petit Paris* museum beside the church, with costumes replicating the famous Durand plantation wedding where the trees in the two-mile approach *allee* were festooned with spider webs sprayed with silver and gold dust. There also remains that undeniably romantic air about St. Martinville, and an obvious determination to prevail despite disasters like the 1855 yellow fever epidemic that wiped out much of the population, the horrific fire in

called the development of St. Martinville in the 1800s "the blooming of a hothouse plant without counterpart on the American continent . . . a pretty little village full of barons, marquises, counts, and countesses," who held great balls and attended theatrical performances and Italian operas. In short, early St. Martinville was presented as "pomp in a bandbox: men in court attire, women in wigs and costly jewelry."

"Emphatically not!" says Dr. Carl Brasseaux, contemporary scholar and one of the world's leading experts on all things Acadian, who insists in his recent book *Acadiana* that the French royalists of "local lore" were of rather more modest socioeconomic backgrounds,

Above: Downtown St. Martinville
Opposite page: Bayou Teche

1856 that would have caused even more damage on Main Street had not a bucket brigade been formed by attendees rushing from the ballet in the Opera House, and the hurricanes that destroyed crops and cattle. St. Martinville would survive, and would do it with charm and grace. And if the barons in court attire and the countesses in fancy wigs never danced the minuets here except in dreams, they certainly *should* have, for this is magical, mythical St. Martinville. *New York Times* bestselling crime writer James Lee Burke, native of nearby New Iberia, today writes wistfully about the nineteenth-century frame buildings with balconies and wood colonnades whose soft decay only add to the aesthetic ambience of the square.

A more down-to-earth picture of life for the majority of the St. Martinville area's population in the early days is presented just a mile south of the historic downtown district at Longfellow-Evangeline State Historic Site, which in 1934 became the first park in the Louisiana state parks system. Through its various components, the park relates the story of settlement patterns and daily life on the early Attakapas district *vacheries* that supplied beef for New Orleans markets.

When in 1755 the British arrested and expelled the French farmers and fishermen from *L'Acadie* (now Nova Scotia), confiscated property, burned homes and boats, and dispersed the populace to the winds in East Coast colonies, Caribbean islands, and Europe, not all were included in the initial wave of evacuation, and not all went peacefully. Some organized resistance to the cruel removal of what the British considered "unassimilable bastions of French popery," according to Dr. Brasseaux, to make way for good loyal Protestant subjects. One respected resistance leader was Joseph "Beausoleil" Broussard, who eventually led a group of Acadian exiles to Louisiana by way of Saint-Domingue. Once in Louisiana, these were sent by the colonial government to the broad grasslands of the Attakapas district.

Helping to guide these exiles was wealthy Creole Hughes Olivier de Vezin, who established the *vacherie* upon lands now comprising the state park. In the early 1800s he built a classic raised Creole cottage, the lower floor of brick made from Bayou Teche clay, the upper floor of *bousillage* (mud-and-moss or -horsehair insulation) between cypress uprights. The main house is surrounded by small dependencies, and other simpler structures depict typical early Acadian homes, with rustic cypress furnishings, outdoor kitchens, and bread ovens. Visitor center exhibits flesh out the picture of early life here with a worn wooden cotton press and a moss cleaner, an Acadian loom and a cypress dugout pirogue.

Further exploring the Acadian experience are several museums behind St. Martin de Tours Church Square. The St. Martinville Cultural Heritage Center contains the Museum of the Acadian Memorial, as well as an African-American Museum recognizing the trials and tribulations of another disenfranchised and oppressed population. In fact, before the arrival of the Acadians, there were black and possibly Native American slaves already present in this area, four of them homesteading and tending cattle on Dauterive's *vacherie*; the first acts in surviving church records for the Attakapas District record the baptisms and marriages of slaves, performed in 1756 by a visiting Catholic priest. A number of Senegambian slaves were sent to the French colony of Louisiana. Those from St. Louis and Goree Island possessed the agricultural skills to successfully cultivate food and cash crops in the tropical heat, an enormously important contribution to early survival. Colonial law provided the means for some of these industrious slaves to obtain their freedom, hence the St. Martinville area had a prosperous class of formerly enslaved farmers, tradesmen, and businessmen.

A shady boardwalk promenade along Bayou Teche, starting at the Evangeline Oak Park and landscaped with labeled native plants and trees, connects the St. Martinville Cultural Heritage Center with the Acadian Memorial. Here a bronze Wall of Names honors the three thousand Acadian refugees who resettled in Louisiana, and in the courtyard are an Eternal Flame and Deportation Cross. The Memorial building is dominated by a colorful thirty-foot audio-interactive mural, "The Arrival of the Acadians in Louisiana," by artist Robert Dafford. Direct descendants of some of the depicted exiles posed for their ancestors' images, and today Cajun families come here to explore their roots in the comprehensive collection of historical records.

Among St. Martinville festivals celebrating area history and traditions is the springtime Acadian Memorial Festival, with music, food, wooden boats, French theater, lectures, and re-enactors arriving along the bayou in mid-1700s period costumes. Another fun festival commemorating

the early customs of the Acadians is *La Grand Boucherie*, held the Saturday before Mardi Gras, with Cajun and Zydeco music, arts and crafts, food, and the butchering of a pig. In the days before refrigeration, only so much fresh meat could be consumed before it spoiled, so only one family killed a pig at any one time, sharing the meat and the work of preserving it with friends and neighbors who, with customary Cajun *joie de vivre*, turned the butchering day into a work/party called a *boucherie*.

The stark realism of life for the early Acadian immigrants is told at the state park and in the museums, but the romantic version, the version that touches the heart— only a poet could do justice to that. In 1847 distinguished American poet Henry Wadsworth Longfellow told the wrenching story of *Le Grand Dérangement* in a poem of epic proportion called "Evangeline."

In the poem, seventeen-year-old Evangeline is separated from her betrothed Gabriel on their wedding day, forced onto separate ships and scattered like flakes of windblown snow. There follows a lifetime of wandering as Evangeline searches for Gabriel, "bleeding, barefooted, over the shards and thorns of existence," across mountains and prairies and finally into the "golden sun, the lakes of Atchafalaya," to hear the "whoop of the crane and the roar of the grim alligator." Upon reaching the banks of the Teche, its oaks garlanded with Spanish moss, "the Eden of Louisiana," she narrowly misses her beloved, and finds him again only upon his deathbed in a poorhouse where she, a Sister of Mercy, comforts the wretched victims. A fleeting kiss, and the lovers reunite at last only in their "nameless graves."

Longfellow based his story on the account of a French-Canadian parishioner of a Maine clergyman, who repeated the tale of separated lovers at a New England dinner party with Nathaniel Hawthorne in 1844; Longfellow himself had never visited Louisiana and had seen the Mississippi River only in a Boston exhibit of a three-mile canvas mural that turned on cylinders to give spectators the feeling of traveling down the river.

His story had several later incarnations, including the rather misguided 1888 novel *Pouponne et Balthazar* by French Creole writer Mme. Sidonie de la Houssaye who recast the characters as upper-class Creoles. In a 1907 version written by St. Martinville legislator Judge Felix Voorhies called *Acadian Reminiscenses: The True Story of the Acadians*, the characters were renamed Emmeline Labiche (said to have been adopted by Voorhies' grandmother in L'Acadie at an early age) and Louis Arceneaux, who reunite beneath a live oak on the banks of Bayou Teche. Alas, Louis has married another, and the heartbroken Emmeline soon seeks the solace of the grave.

Through the years the different versions of the story were told and retold, touching the hearts of listeners, exciting the imaginations of the storytellers, until the details of the different versions mixed and mingled, and they were told and heard so often with such heartfelt emotion that they came to be believed, even revered, with Evangeline assuming the status of a saint, albeit a secular one.

Like author Harnett Kane, who never allowed the

Opposite page: Evangeline Oak

limitations of cold hard fact to stand in the way of a colorful story, St. Martinville embraced Evangeline/Emmeline as its own, and when the mists rise from the muddy waters of Bayou Teche to surround the Evangeline Oak, it matters not that other trees have carried the same designation. Nor does it matter that there is no body in the tomb at Evangeline's Monument beside St. Martin de Tours Catholic Church because there was no Evangeline, nor that the statue of Evangeline is not Evangeline but Dolores del Rio, a Mexican film star who played the role in the 1920s Hollywood silent film.

It matters not, for this is stuff that myth is made of. The lovers, real or not, stood for something larger than their own stories; they symbolized the sorrow and the longing for lost community as well as the enduring strength and will to survive of the Acadians dispersed throughout the world, especially those who managed to come together again in Louisiana. Dr. Brasseaux notes that Evangeline's story, however told, helps focus attention on all those "unsung survivors who stubbornly braved adversity, oppression, and separation to carve a Louisiana homeland for themselves and their progeny."

So bravo for St. Martinville's celebration of the lovers and their landmarks, mythological or not, and long may contemporary romantics reunite at the Evangeline Oak each Valentine's Day or hold wedding services in the gazebo sheltered by the old oak. The fancy French royalists of *Le Petit Paris* have embraced an unpretentious little Acadian girl and, in the end, made her enduring story their own.

Today the economy of the area relies heavily on sugarcane and crawfish, both wild ones harvested from the Atchafalaya Basin and millions of pounds harvested from ponds. Guided swamp tours introduce entranced visitors to the beauties of the Atchafalaya, America's largest river-basin swamp. Birders find the country's largest wading bird rookery in nearby Lake Martin, the nests easily visible from walkways around the lake but even more impressive on boat tours; the lake has a large population of huge alligators as well. Besides La Grande Boucherie and the Acadian festivals, other fun gatherings celebrate peppers and okra, and it goes without saying that there are some fine restaurants and cafés serving up great Cajun cuisine.

Since St. Martinville became a Main Street community in 1993, the program has used its funding and façade grants to preserve the town's unique character and charm, restoring and renovating so as to enhance rather than detract from what makes St. Martinville so special. The Main Street manager says her favorite downtown festival is the St. Lucy Festival of Lights and the Knights of Columbus Christmas Parade, because, she says, St. Lucy is the patron saint of the eyes, and downtown St. Martinville is a veritable feast for the eyes. And so it is.

Slidell

Population: 27,068

Without undertaking a costly and perilous ocean voyage, goods being transported northward from New Orleans in the nineteenth century had to either take a riverboat up the Mississippi or ferry across Lake Pontchartrain to slog through the Honey Island Swamp. What a welcome relief, then, was the construction in the 1880s of the New Orleans and Northeastern Railroad connecting the Crescent City with Meridian, Mississippi, with its first work camp on the North Shore established on the high ground that today is Slidell.

Large landowner Baron Frederick Erlanger, a financier who headed the banking syndicate financing the railroad construction, is credited with founding Slidell in 1883 and naming it for his illustrious father-in-law, statesman and international diplomat John Slidell. An attorney and businessman who was born in New York and moved to New Orleans in 1819, Slidell represented the area in both houses of the U.S. Congress. He served as Commissioner to Mexico with instructions to settle the Texas-Mexico boundary dispute, then represented the Confederacy in France in a futile effort to gain military support during the Civil War. Disappointed by the failure of his mission there, Slidell remained abroad until his death.

The original plans for the city were drawn by Col. Leon J. Fremaux, Louisiana engineer and planter, who laid out the streets in a grid pattern, the north-south ones mostly numbered and the east-west ones named for himself, Erlanger, and the railroad's chief engineering officer, G. Bouscaren. Col. Fremaux was an illustrious New Orleans character who served during the Civil War as Gen. P. G. T. Beauregard's topographical engineer and laid out the defense of Port Hudson, the last Confederate stronghold on the Mississippi; he was famous for his wartime sketches and was also a recognized sculptor and engraver.

Slidell was formally incorporated in 1888, and by 1890 had a population of 364. The coming of the railroad proved a real catalyst for growth, opening the door for other industries dependent upon it for transportation. Soon there was a shipyard and a large lumber mill; the plentiful virgin cypress logged from the Pearl River Swamp was hauled along light rail lines to the sawmill. Stores, hotels, and saloons popped up on Front Street to service the growing community. The St. Joe Brickworks, one of the country's largest brick manufacturers, began as the Fritz Salmen Brickyard and employed so many workers that there was a two-story general mercantile store where employees could spend the scrip given as pay.

A large creosote plant, built around 1910, burned five years later with great loss of life; it was very sensibly rebuilt

closer to a fire station and a water source, which ironically proved to be disastrous when the creosote polluted the bayou—the source of much of the community's drinking water. In the late 1990s the plant site was cleaned up under the Environmental Protection Agency Superfund program, the canal dredged, and the waste incinerated. Today the restored site serves as Heritage Park and a community playground, with open spaces for ballgames, concert venues, and a boat launch, plus fishing on the bayou.

While the railroad remains an important influence in Slidell (Amtrak's Crescent connects with major points from New Orleans to New York, its station on Front Street in Olde Towne Slidell is in view of Heritage Park), the intersections of major new interstate highways have turned the city into a busy crossroads community. This is especially true given its proximity to New Orleans (crime and blight having sent a huge number of New Orleanians scurrying "across the lake") and to a number of NASA space facilities, including the Michoud Assembly Facility in New Orleans and the John C. Stennis Space Center in nearby Bay St. Louis. Slidell's population more than tripled beginning in the 1960s and '70s with the advent of the U.S. space program, and today it is a major regional retail center and home to more than thirty thousand people.

Slidell is also the location of the National Weather Service forecast office for the Greater New Orleans/Baton Rouge metropolitan areas. Consequently, in August 2005, the ominous growing intensity of Hurricane Katrina was viewed from there with enormous trepidation, and on August 29 Slidell was inundated by a catastrophic storm surge ranging between ten and sixteen feet, some places even higher. Damage was extensive.

And yet Slidell has continued to grow, and now there is a concerted effort to revitalize Olde Towne to preserve the earliest section of town. One of the more recent additions to the state Main Street program, Slidell also received accreditation into the National Trust Main Street program, recognizing it as a strong revitalization effort using the four-point approach to strengthen the local economy and protect its historic buildings. The accreditation recognized the strong community support here for the commercial district revitalization and the involvement of both public and private sectors in the effort. "The citizens of Slidell have been very consistent in voicing their belief in keeping

the heart and history of their city alive, and have also volunteered countless hours to the effort over the years," says the Main Street manager.

One of the Main Street program's priorities has been to bring human resources together through a new organizational structure, overseen by an executive board called "Friends of Olde Towne Slidell," or FOOTS. Despite economic challenges, according to the program manager, Olde Towne shows definite signs of progress, and the opening of the city's Cultural and Technology Center administration building plus its auditorium promise to bring hundreds of city employees to the area, with the increased traffic creating all sorts of positive possibilities. A number of fine eateries draw patrons to Olde Towne (iconic chef John Besh grew up in Slidell), and there are

artists' studios, cigar shops, bicycle shops, printing and food stores, bakeries, magazine headquarters, and an interesting mix of other small businesses bringing unique character and flavor to the area.

One large renovation project in Olde Towne that successfully applied tax abatements was the returning of the old Champagne building to its original charm, an ambitious project that enhanced the appearance of an entire block of Carey Street. Another major renovation involves the old brick Minicappelli Building, once nearly destroyed in a disastrous fire, but now planning to bring new life to the corner of First and Cousin. The Main Street program installed dozens of festive blue and green banners and also added white lights around several hundred St. Charles poles to identify and illuminate Olde Towne's main commercial areas. Working toward a more pedestrian and bike-friendly district with great visual appeal and enhanced landscaping, the Main Street manager has worked closely with the Regional Planning Commission on a Transportation Enhancement Project of nearly $1 million for improving curbs, sidewalks, streetscapes, parking, and crosswalks in the heart of Olde Towne.

Main Street Slidell has also received a grant for the reviewing and updating of historic district ordinances, with a state-sponsored resource team of professionals leading a citizen-based data- and best practices-driven planning process that will guide future development while protecting the health, safety, and welfare of the community. In terms of historic preservation and revitalization, the Main

Time Out Lounge in a rehabbed pharmacy building

Street program in Slidell provides the structure, support, expertise, training, and tools needed to get it right. "The network is there to open doors and minds about changes that will determine the future of Olde Towne's economic viability," says the manager of the program.

The Slidell Historic Antique District in Olde Town has dozens of dealers, primarily along First and Erlanger Streets. Special events draw residents and tourists alike to enjoy the historic charm of Antique Row, old homes, and small businesses. Spring and fall Antique District street fairs draw plenty of visitors and vendors, and there are fall Arts Evenings featuring live entertainment and the works of more than one hundred artists. The Slidell Museum has an assortment of exhibits in the 1907 Town Hall and Jail. The structure, built to replace the original wooden one, served as town hall until 1954; the town fire engine was parked in an addition.

Bordering Lake Pontchartrain and the Honey Island Swamp, the Slidell area offers a wealth of recreational water sports and fascinating swamp tours, plus Mardi Gras parades and balls, the St. Tammany Parish Trade Fair, and other fun festivals. And yet, in the shadow of the space program and the hustle and bustle of modern developments surrounding it, Olde Towne Slidell remains a little island of tranquility and a reminder of Slidell's history and heritage, which must not be forgotten. "Experience Olde Towne" is the Main Street program's message to the hurried and harried of today; step back into the quiet charm of a unique piece of the past that is today experiencing renewed economic vitality.

Above: Arcade Theatre
Below: Downtown Slidell

Springhill

Population: 5,269

Northernmost of Louisiana's Main Street communities, sitting right on the Arkansas border, Springhill is a small town with big aspirations, not to mention the state's biggest single-screen cinema showing first-run movies every night of the week. It also has the dogged determination and perseverance to endure the ups and downs of a fluctuating economy dependent over the years mainly on the timber industry.

Situated in the middle of lush pine forests, Springhill was first and most appropriately known as Piney Woods after the families of William Farmer, Samuel Monzingo, J. A. Byrnes, and Joseph Murrell first homesteaded in the area in the mid-1800s. A sawmill town with twenty-five company homes arose after the arrival of the Bodcaw Lumber Company in 1894. Bodcaw had some fifty employees, and the wife of one of them christened the town Barefoot due to the number of men working without shoes.

It was said that around Christmas 1896, the secretary and commissary manager for the new Pine Woods Lumber Company, J. F. Giles, turned over the Barefoot Station sign and wrote **Springhill** on the other side. Early Springhill had a company store, post office, and a barber shop. A railroad line soon extended from Stamps, Arkansas. The town was incorporated in 1902, and the sawmill's big dynamo provided the only electricity until Louisiana Power and Light came to town in 1927.

Dr. Sam Williamson, introducing a book of local history, paints a poignant word picture appealing to all the senses as he describes life in this small sawmill town over the years: "the grinding of sawmill machinery on a summer night, the pungent odor from the paper mill on a wet evening, the rumble of heavy oil rigs moving through town . . ."

The Great Depression brought the beginnings of

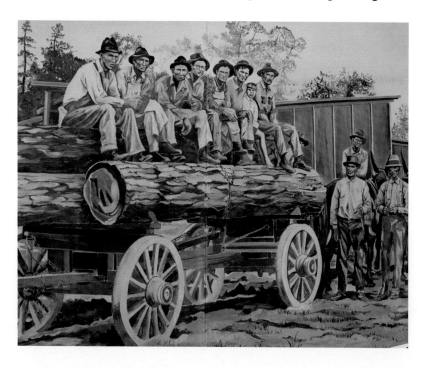

Springhill's ups and downs with the lumber business, an association so all-pervasive that the high school athletic teams were for many years called the Lumberjacks. Pine Woods Lumber Company closed after thirty-six years in operation. The mill was subsequently purchased and operated by Frost Lumber Company, then Springhill Lumber Company, and then Anthony Forest Products Company. In 1937 International Paper Company opened a large Kraft paper mill, later augmented by a box plant, employing so many new residents (850 the first year of operation) that a number of its employees lived in tents in what is now Springhill City Park. The IP payroll was a multi-million dollar boost to the local economy, and the growing community of Springhill became an important manufacturing and processing center for North Louisiana.

When IP closed its paper mill in the late 1970s, the sons and grandsons of the builders of the mill sadly helped to demolish it. International Paper's wood products plant was sold to rival Georgia Pacific and is no longer in operation, but IP has two divisions operating today, the Springhill Container Division making corrugated shipping containers and the Springhill Converting Operation that converts bulk paper into posters and other special orders. Today Tucker Lumber has a new sawmill, plus a crosstie trimming and end-plate plant. Oil and gas activity in the area over the years has had as many ups and downs as the timber industry, most recently a frenzied "up" in this Haynesville Shale region of northwest Louisiana; the first gas-producing well was brought in in 1918.

Several National Scenic Waterways surround Springhill. Dorcheat Bayou to the east and Bodcau Bayou to the west, plus Lake Erling to the north, provide great fishing, boating, and other water sports. Nearby sections of Kisatchie National Forest, Bodcau Wildlife Management Area, and other preserved woodlands provide plenty of rolling hills and piney woods for hiking, camping, hunting, birdwatching, and all sorts of recreational activities for outdoor enthusiasts. Springhill also boasts one of the state's largest outdoor rodeo arenas, which hosts an annual Professional Rodeo Cowboys' Association rodeo each June.

But the center of life in Springhill is its historic Main Street commercial corridor, which in spite of economic downturns is being revitalized with aesthetic improvements, new businesses, and even a renovated library. Springhill became a Louisiana Main Street community in 1997, and since then the program has

expended much effort in providing support and matching funding for the varied businesses occupying the historic structures here. In addition to the Willie Mack Memorial Library, Main Street is home to banks, insurance agencies and attorneys, beauty salons and health care providers, a radio station, financial services, jewelers and florists, clothing boutiques and home centers, cleaners and travel agencies, fire department and motor vehicles office. There's a Mexican restaurant and a colorful little ice cream parlor, and the Springhill Art League showcases original art works. In short, Springhill residents today can pretty well take care of all their business right on Main Street just as they did in the early days.

The pride of the Springhill historic downtown area is the restored Spring Theatre. How many little towns can

boast of nightly movies? Like Springhill itself, the Spring Theatre has endured its ups and downs. It was built in 1946 by the Tri-State Theater Company but burned down in 1958. What was left of the structure was purchased by Boyd Adkison, who reopened the Spring in 1958 and then died of cancer the following year. His widow remarried and ran the theater for another couple of decades until she too passed away in 1982.

The Spring Theatre's proudest moment was in 1979, when actor George Peppard, then married to a Springhill native, premiered his film *Five Days From Home* about a Louisiana prison inmate's escape in an attempt to reach his ailing son's bedside on the West Coast. During the 1980s the theater was briefly used as a church, then fell into disrepair. After private donors purchased the facility and generously gave it to the city of Springhill, a

partnership was struck in 2002 between Boyd Adkison's son and Adam Harris, who began the enormous task of completely renovating the theater. Harris worked around the clock, occasionally sleeping overnight in the theater, until the 415-seat auditorium was beautifully renovated, with a 40x20-foot screen (the largest single screen in the state except for IMAX theatres) and state-of-the-art sound. Harris and his wife, now sole owners, have received the thanks and support of the entire community, and the Spring Theatre has been named the North Webster Chamber of Commerce's Outstanding Business of the Year. There's only one showing nightly, so everybody in town is there, and there are special cut rates for seniors and children.

Springhill's Main Street, with its eye-catching clock tower, hosts a number of special events and festivities throughout the year, all designed to make the historic district a fun place for visitors and profitable for its retail businesses. Mardi Gras and Christmas parades pass along this historic corridor, as does the Lumberjack Festival Parade in October, part of the area's most popular festival for three decades, featuring a car show (street rods, classic, and antique cars), an antique tractor and engine show, big-name musical entertainment, food, arts and crafts vendors, and a great children's corner. In November each year, Main to Main Trade Days line the highways of Webster Parish from Springhill Main Street to downtown Minden with garage sales and food vendors. And the Springhill Main Street's Christmas on Main features photos and visits with Santa at AmJenn's Soups & Scoops, plus stretch limo and hummer rides around the historic district, refreshments, and musical entertainment in the new Frank B. Anthony Park.

The events are carefully planned to fulfill Springhill Main Street's goal of bringing shoppers back to a revitalized commercial corridor with renovated historic structures housing retail outlets that are fun to browse through and shop in. Says the Main Street manager, "The businesses in the district are concentrating their efforts toward creating an atmosphere that is conducive to the quality of life desired by residents and visitors alike. It is about bringing a thriving community together to enjoy the relaxed pace of friendly country living, yet still be a part of all the festivals, parades, and many activities and opportunities around us." In spring and summer, Main Street sponsors a popular farmers' market and joins in community clean-up campaigns and other activities as well.

With standing committees comprised of downtown stakeholders including business and property owners, employees, residents, and community leaders, Springhill Main Street applies a comprehensive approach relying on quality to make meaningful long-term revitalization

possible through public and private partnerships by focusing on existing assets and encouraging new development.

This Main Street approach has generated a revived sense of place in historic downtown Springhill, this little community with big dreams and an admirable and unfailing resiliency. As the slogans say, Springhill is special indeed.

Thibodaux

Population: 14,566

Along this scenic bayou where the waters of the Mighty Mississippi once flowed to the Gulf, called on early maps the *Districto de La Fourche de Los Chetimachas*, the earliest inhabitants were Native Americans of the Chitimacha tribe, their cypress dugout canoes slipping silently along the waterways that were the early highways. Soon they were joined by European explorers, French and Canadians like Iberville and Bienville in the late 1600s. As this colonial frontier shifted from French to Spanish control and then back again, land grants were made to Canary Islanders and German immigrants seeking a new life in the New World, and to French Acadians cruelly ousted from Nova Scotia, their little cypress cabins filled with dozens of stair-step children and built so close together that the first bayouside highway, LA 1, became known as the longest street in the world.

With the Louisiana Purchase in 1803, Anglo-Americans arrived, often accompanied by African and Caribbean slaves, to establish the large sugar plantations on the fertile lands along the bayou, fields enriched by nutrient-laden floodwaters every spring. Each culture left its footprint on Lafourche's rich soil, but it would be a New Yorker named Henry Schuyler Thibodeaux, landowner, legislator, and short-time interim state governor, who founded the city that took his name when he made available several tracts of land for a courthouse and market.

From these tracts the village of Thibodeauxville, later Thibodeaux and finally Thibodaux, spread out from Bayou Lafourche into a compact, dense city center, its narrow streets today still lined with the historic buildings that formed the commercial heart of the Lafourche district, an important port and trading post in the early 1800s. Along the bayou came flatboats and small steamers from the Ohio River and the Midwest, loaded with corn, meat, potatoes, apples, whiskey, and flour to trade for local crops of sugar, molasses, cotton, rice, and moss.

In 1808 Thibodaux became the seat of government of what was called Lafourche Interior, a sprawling parish that initially included property later separated as Terrebonne Parish. The town was incorporated in 1838 during the governorship of Judge Edward Douglas White, one of three native sons to hold that high office. Its muddy streets were lined with *banquettes* made of flatboat gunwales. When a contract was let for a ferry crossing the bayou in 1847, with a skiff for foot passengers and a sturdy flatboat that could hold four horses at a time, the charges were five cents per person or horse or horned cow, four cents for sheep or hog, and forty or fifty cents for two-wheeled carriages. Ministers and militia crossed free of charge.

Late nineteenth-century journalist Martha R. Fields described Thibodaux as a "fitting metropolis of a district like that of Lafourche . . . the best managed, the cleanest and neatest town in the state, laid out with the regularity of a chess board. First-class shops and a large bank are practical evidence of progress, several factory industries, boiler works, an ice factory, two good newspapers, two fire companies, a theater, churches including the finest Catholic Church outside New Orleans, excellent schools and a refined and cultured social life."

Southern portions of Lafourche Parish, "*down de bayou*," lived off the largesse of the coastal marshes and swamps, wetlands richly blessed with an abundance of fish and other seafood to be caught and fur-bearing animals to be trapped and hunted. But along the upper reaches of the bayou, sugar was king. In good years Lafourche sugar planters produced more than a million tons of cane.

Today visitors can get a feel for the enormity of sugarcane's importance at Laurel Valley Plantation, dating from the 1770s, one of the most complete collections of original dependencies and outbuildings in the state, a cabinscape of some sixty structures characteristic of antebellum southern plantations. Orderly rows of weathered and worn cypress cabins once housed the huge labor force required to keep this giant sugar plantation running smoothly. Today their tin roofs are rusted and their porch steps caving in. The surrounding fields are still planted with cane, but the workers' quarters stand silent and empty now, machinery having replaced the mule and plow, the field hand and hoe. In the old plantation store, exhibits tell the workers' stories, recalling the days when they were paid as little as $13 a month, often in scrip redeemable only at the company store. In November 1887 Thibodaux was the scene of a labor strike right at the onset of the crucial grinding period; it resulted in a shameful massacre of dozens, maybe even hundreds, of mostly black cane workers.

Vast acreages are still planted in cane and there are still operational mills in the upper parish, while along the coast fisheries and the energy industry take precedence. In the 1930s, Lower Lafourche was transformed into a Wild West boomtown with the discovery of oil. Port Fourchon today is home to the largest Gulf support base for offshore oil and gas services, vital to the nation's energy supply. But just as the cane crop was at the mercy of late freezes, hurricanes, and crop diseases, so the oil industry has been susceptible to fluctuations in price and demand,

Oil & Gas Building

making the oilfield a gambler's paradise just as much as the sugar plantation ever was. The Thibodaux area has seen boom times and busts, and at just thirteen feet above sea level has certainly had its share of disastrous hurricanes as well. It perseveres nonetheless.

As this parish celebrated its 200th anniversary in 2007, local newspaperman John DeSantis, writing in a special edition of the *Daily Comet*, called Thibodaux and Lafourche Parish places where "the past and present are wrapped so comfortably in each other's arms that it's hard to see where one ends and the other begins," where cypress trawlers painstakingly handcrafted by French-speaking shrimpers ply bayou waters beside modern multi-million-dollar high-tech vessel manufacturers like Bollinger Shipyards or Edison Chouest Offshore, and where the echoes of slave chants are drowned out in the cane fields by the roar of modern machinery.

Today, downtown Thibodaux remains a vital part of life here, its streets numbered from Bayou Lafourche where LA 1 parallels the waterway. The central focus is the large, bustling Lafourche Parish Courthouse, which dates from 1861. Designed by noted New Orleans architect Henry Howard and topped by a massive copper dome, it originally

Dansereau House

Lafourche Parish Courthouse

faced Second Street; now its entrance portico with four massive fluted columns faces Green Street. Howard's partner Henri Thiberge designed the Dansereau House, located at Philip Street at Fifth Street. It was the medical office of Dr. Hercules Dansereau and now is a popular inn complete with arch-head windows, six-sided cupola, ornate balustrade, and bracketed cornices. On Third Street the old parish jail, originally a Gothic fortress with a hanging chamber, houses government offices.

On Seventh Street are several of the most significant religious edifices in Thibodaux: St. John's Episcopal Church, St. Joseph's Co-Cathedral, and Calvary United Methodist Church. St. John's, a rare example of Georgian church architecture, is considered the oldest Episcopal

Nicholls"). The impressive Renaissance Romanesque St. Joseph Co-Cathedral was built in 1923. Patterned after European cathedrals with elaborate frescoes, vaulted ceilings, and magnificent stained glass, the cathedral also contains a sacred relic of St. Valerie, Christian martyr beheaded in second-century Rome. When an earlier St. Joseph's burned in 1916, St. Valerie's reliquary was rescued by local volunteer firemen in an act of heroism celebrated each year during the immensely popular and long established Fireman's Fair and parade that supports the city's 450-plus volunteer fire department. Nearby is the Calvary United Methodist Church, formed in 1867 as one of the area's earliest black religious, educational, and social centers.

The Lafourche Heritage Society prints detailed maps for walking tours through this historic downtown district, which is filled with both commercial and residential

St. John's Episcopal Church

church west of the Mississippi River and dates from the early 1840s, when it was established by Bishop Leonidas Polk of nearby Leighton Plantation; in its peaceful oak-shaded cemetery rest a number of Thibodaux legends, including two-term governor Francis T. Nicholls, for whom the local university was named (a brigadier general who lost an arm and foot in battle, Nicholls' nomination for governor was for "all that is left of Francis Tillou

Iron Balconies

designed by the Main Street program to encourage the enjoyment of Thibodaux's historic downtown district are the annual Downtown Thibodaux Arts Walk in the spring and the Big Boy's Main Street Cook-Off in November. Thibodaux Main Street also sponsors a farmer's market on the grounds of Jean Lafitte National Park on Saturdays during the spring and fall growing seasons.

Other festivals like Jean Lafitte National Park's fall *Fête d'Ecologie* celebrate the region's Cajun culture, with arts and crafts, demonstrations of old-time skills, food, live music, and dancing. The Thibodeauxville Fall Festival even has a duck race on the bayou, while the spring Jubilee Arts & Humanities Festival and the Louisiana Swamp Stomp at Nicholls both celebrate all manner of artistic endeavors

structures varying in architectural design from Victorian, Queen Anne, or Creole cottages to Vieux Carre style with lacy iron balconies and second-story living spaces above first-floor retail storefronts. Within the compact central core of downtown are boutique shops and antiques stores, some upscale restaurants and lively bars popular with local college students, attorneys' offices, a library, and a number of other viable businesses.

When Thibodaux became a Main Street community in 2009, the program contributed its incentive grants and other support to join with existing private and governmental preservation and economic development groups to encourage the revitalization of the historic downtown area. Among the most popular of local events

Downtown Thibodaux

with dozens of events. Thibodaux has a Christmas parade, and Mardi Gras balls and parades provide a final exuberant fling before the austerity of Lenten season in this predominantly Catholic community. There are swamp tours by boat and airboat conducted by knowledgeable professional alligator hunters and fishermen showcasing the richness of the surrounding wetlands, and several plantation homes in the area welcome visitors for tours, including the 1825 home of Gov. E. D. White, now a state historic site.

Along Bayou Lafourche at the edge of the downtown district, Jean Lafitte National Park's Wetlands Acadian Cultural Center is an interpretive center offering performances and demonstrations, bayou boat trips, jam sessions for local musicians, guided walking tours, and compelling exhibits explaining the heartbreak of *Le Grand Dérangement* that wrenched thousands of French farmers and fishermen from English-controlled L'Acadie on the Canadian coast and flung them throughout the world. Their resilience in the face of disaster can be seen throughout the Thibodaux region today, the world having come to understand and appreciate the music and cuisine, the crafts and customs, the dances and the irrepressible

Paddling on the Bayou Lafourche

joie de vivre of these hardy souls called Cajuns.

Parallels can be drawn between the Acadians and many of the small Main Street communities like Thibodaux, such as resiliency in the face of trials, tribulations, and tragedies, determination to persevere, and they are pictures of the past that can and should be preserved by finding present-day meaning and fiscal viability.

Winnsboro

Population: 4,910

"An inspiring example of what can happen when a community believes in itself and the value of the arts to quality of life." That sparkling tribute was paid to one of Winnsboro's proudest reclamation achievements upon receipt of a Governor's Arts Award, but it actually applies to the entire Main Street program there. Working with an active Historic Preservation Commission and Board of Directors, the community-driven Main Street initiative in Winnsboro strives to improve economic management, strengthen public participation, and make its preserved downtown a fun place to be. And what is the key to its success, according to the dynamic and determined Main Street manager? "I will say, with no bull, it's the people. It really is! Our architecture isn't really spectacular, we don't have a river running through us or a charming university. It's the people. Pretty special, if I do say so."

Even without a river or charming college, however, Winnsboro's Main Street, called Prairie Street, is a brilliant little jewel of a preserved commercial corridor, its buildings

carefully restored and well maintained, its businesses bustling with patrons, its public spaces providing stimulating exhibits and programs and just plain fun. Visitors can tell how special the experience here will be the minute they turn off the state highway leading into town, the inviting entrance beautifully landscaped with flags flying, the ornamental iron signage providing just a hint of the spectacular shopping opportunities that await in small businesses with enticing names like Sweet Pea's, Every Occasion, and Painted Pony.

Although it was founded back in the 1840s as the seat of government for Franklin Parish, many of Winnsboro's downtown commercial structures date from soon after the village was incorporated in 1902. The real gem in the downtown crown is the Princess Theatre, in a building constructed in 1907. Opened as a vaudeville house in 1912, the Princess in 1925 became a theater showing

silent movies, with rousing accompaniment by a live in-house pianist. With the advent of talkies, a sound system was installed by theater operator George Elam.

Competition from multiplex movie houses in the region led to the closing of the Princess Theatre in the late 1980s, followed by a period of dormancy until 1992, when the Ramage family, longtime owners, generously donated it to the city of Winnsboro. An ambitious renovation began the following year, and by 1994 the Princess reopened its doors to welcome the children and grandchildren of many of its original patrons to experience the magic of the theater for themselves.

The restoration received the Governor's Arts Award in 2002, which commended it for being "the catalyst for the development of historic downtown Winnsboro," for transforming cultural opportunities in northeast Louisiana, and for providing an exemplary model for success throughout the region. Today the Princess Theatre continues its contribution to the life and economy of Winnsboro by hosting an exciting line-up of musical performances, community theater, dance programs, and exhibits, functioning not just as a performing arts venue but also as a forum for educational programming. The adjacent Princess Room also provides a venue for events. And when the annual patron's night opening of the theater's summer musical somehow always closely follows upon the heels (hooves?) of the annual afternoon rodeo parade with plenty of mounted participants downtown, the hardworking town crew gets to showcase their skillful shovel work and speedy street clean-up skills!

Another significant anchor of historic downtown Prairie Street is the Old Post Office Museum, which dates from 1936. After years of planning and a wonderfully creative renovation, this museum opened its doors to the public in the fall of 2010. Besides exhibit space for revolving art exhibits, the building provides office space for the Winnsboro-Franklin Chamber of Commerce, Winnsboro Main Street, the Franklin Parish Economic Development Foundation, and the Franklin Parish Tourism Commission. The fascinating old vault houses a scrapbook collection compiled by Nell Dailey McLemore covering parish history beginning in the 1940s. Hanging in the lobby is a 6x10-foot Louisiana flag hand-painted by inmates of the Louisiana State Penitentiary at Angola in the 1920s for Gov. Huey P. Long. Nostalgic mailboxes

Old Post Office Museum

can be "rented" to support the museum, especially popular with those who actually received mail in them over the years.

Between these two iconic structures, the Princess and the post office, Prairie Street is lined with a wide variety of small businesses and service providers in tidy little buildings, many with colorful awnings streetside—realtors and office supply companies, salons and dentists, the public library and newspaper office, antiques and gift shops, banks and shoe repair shops, attorneys and cleaners, and shops displaying the latest fashions. Kinloch Plantation Pecan Oil, the healthy 100 percent virgin pecan oil with no additives, preservatives, or stabilizers, is called the most heart-healthy oil available and is manufactured on Prairie Street. An upscale bed and breakfast, the Jackson Street Guest House, provides luxury accommodations in the historic district adjacent to the Franklin Parish Courthouse, and whimsical murals by local artist Margaret Ellerman liven up the brick sides of the *Franklin Sun* building and the old Catfish Festival office next to City Hall.

Since Winnsboro became a Main Street community in 1987, close to one hundred new businesses have been created, adding hundreds of new jobs and millions of dollars in private and public investment. Although the Main Street philosophy here is interpreted so as to have a positive effect community-wide, the program works closely with the local Chamber of Commerce and Tourism Commission to assist its downtown historic district merchants in receiving special grant opportunities and

tax advantages for renovation and restoration of vintage commercial structures. Main Street maintains a presence on the boards of most local and parish historical and

development organizations, sponsors business seminars and educational workshops for downtown merchants, and has had a hand in a number of tangible improvements—

enlarging the historic district, purchasing picturesque new streetlights, implementing the memorial iron bench project, and restoring downtown murals.

The Main Street program here also takes an active role in sponsoring and supporting special events. Hot August Night is a much anticipated fundraiser, a gala featuring music, food, and art, while Prairie Street Prowl and Scarecrows in Town provide lots of fun for children downtown during Halloween. During the statewide Main to Main celebrations the first full weekend in November, "Found on 15" transforms the length of Hwy. 15 through Franklin Parish (from Big Creek to Big Dan's) into a giant twenty-five-mile yard sale that attracts shoppers from miles around. Christmas season lets Winnsboro show off spectacular lighting and decorations downtown with a big evening parade and great shopping. Other events called Pickin' on Prairie and Pickin' in the Park feature area musicians.

But the premier special event here for a quarter of a century has been the enormously popular Franklin Parish Catfish Festival, annually attracting some twenty thousand fans to listen to live music, browse through hundreds of crafts booths, admire antique cars and special exhibits, and eat more than two tons of fried farm-raised filets here where catfish is king. This is Louisiana's largest one-day festival.

World War II hero Gen. Claire Chennault of the Fighting Tigers had early ties to this patriotic area that bills itself as the Stars and Stripes Capitol of Louisiana. Other notable names associated over the years with Winnsboro have included the estimable Ben Franklin for whom the parish was named, Sen. John Winn for whom the city was named, several famous professional athletes, rock and roll pianist Puddler Harris, and an assortment of contemporary politicians including the illustrious "None of the Above" Knox, perennial candidate who legally changed his name and who, given Louisiana's infamously quirky political scene, probably over the years received a whole lot of votes!

But it's the everyday ordinary people, as the Main Street manager asserts, who really are *extraordinary* and make the little town of Winnsboro what it is, a place with a real feeling of community and caring, where people willingly pitch in to preserve its history and vintage downtown structures to strengthen existing assets while at the same time expanding and diversifying the economic base. This is a little town that obviously cares. It shows. And fortunately the Main Street program here has a veteran manager with well-honed people skills, that enviable ability to forge and sustain coalitions of volunteers and professionals working together and doing it not only willingly and enthusiastically, but, by God, with a smile!

Main Streets . . . Then and Now

Public Domain, Library of Congress Prints and Photographs Division.

Crowley

It took the coming of the railroad to open these flat treeless prairies for settlement, and it took Midwestern farmers to see the potential for growing rice. At one time Crowley milled more of the grain than any other rice-producing area in the world, and its annual fall International Rice Festival still attracts enormous crowds to the wide divided boulevard that remains the center of life in this Rice Capital of the World.

Courtesy of Northwestern State University of Louisiana, Watson Memorial Library, Cammie G. Henry Research Center, Millspaugh Collection of Photography, image 1-09-05.

Natchitoches

Historic Front Street in Natchitoches, oldest permanent European settlement in the Louisiana Purchase, has overlooked the Cane River Lake since the days of horse-drawn vehicles. While they said you could throw a quarter down this old bricked street in the 1970s and never hit a thing, today it attracts multitudes of visitors and locals alike with its lively atmosphere, colorful shops and restaurants, upscale loft living, and a perfect combination of historic preservation with present-day economic vitality.

I. A. Martin Photo Collection, Iberia Parish Library, New Iberia, La.

New Iberia

Founded in the 1770s by a small group of Spanish colonists, New Iberia's historic commercial corridor along the banks of beautiful Bayou Teche has successfully reinvented itself as a nucleus of culture, commerce, and tourism, not to mention the stomping grounds of bedeviled detective Dave Robicheaux in the crime novels of native son and prize-winning author James Lee Burke. What is now the Sliman Theater for the Performing Arts began life in the late nineteenth century as a wholesale grocery that morphed into the Evangeline, its marquee still enlivening this thriving downtown community.

Public Domain, City of Thibodaux, La.

Thibodaux

Its narrow streets are paved today instead of rutted dirt, and the loungers don't wear straw boaters or knickers anymore, but downtown Thibodaux still bustles with life along Bayou Lafourche. By the early 1800s it was an important port and trading post for the surrounding wetlands and rich sugar plantations, besides being the important seat of government. Today this thriving little college town manages to retain its historic charm and lively sense of *joie de vivre*.

Louisiana Main Street
Louisiana Division of Historic Preservation
Office of Cultural Development
Department of Culture, Recreation & Tourism
Box 44247
Baton Rouge, LA 70804
Tel: (225)342-8162
Fax: (225)342-8173
Mainstreet@crt.la.gov
www.louisianahp.org

LOUISIANA
OFFICE OF CULTURAL DEVELOPMENT

MAIN STREET PROGRAM
DEVELOPING OUR CULTURAL ASSETS

Charlene Beckett
Box 1170
Abbeville, LA 70511
(337) 898-4110
abbevillemainstreet@cox-internet.com

Marc Vereen
Box 431
Bastrop, LA 71221
(318) 283-3308
mvereen@cityofbastrop.com

Carol Shirley
8173 Folly Brown Rd.
Clinton, LA 70722
(225) 603-9003
carolshirley@aol.com

Polly Harrelson
Box 10
Columbia, LA 71418
(318) 649-2138
columbiamainstreet@yahoo.com

Alice Clarke
Box 901
Crowley, LA 70526
(337) 788-4123
ali.clarke@crowley-la.com

Donna Jennings
Box 1629
Denham Springs, LA 70727
(225) 667-8308
djennings1@bellsouth.net

Misty Clanton
200 S. Jefferson St.
DeRidder, LA 70634
(337) 462-8900
mclanton@cityofderidder.org

Missy Jandura
Box 346
Donaldsonville, LA 70346
(225) 323-2555
directorddd@gmail.com

Joan McManus
Box 1106
Eunice, LA 70535
(337) 457-6503
eunicela@hotmail.com

Franklin Main Street
300 Iberia St.
Franklin, LA 70538
(337) 828-6326
info@franklin-la.com

Lynn Smith
Box 2788
Hammond, LA 70403
(985) 542-3471
ddd@hammond.org

Anne Picou
317 Goode St.
Houma, LA 70306
(985) 873-6408
apicou@tpcg.org

Sam Kincade
101 West Lee St.
Leesville, LA 71446
(337) 392-1776
leesmainstreet@bellsouth.net

Pattie Odom
520 Broadway
Minden, LA 71055
(318) 371-4258
mainstreet@mindenusa.com

Steve Morrell
Box 1218
Morgan City, LA 70381
(985) 380-4639
mcmainst@yahoo.com

Lisa Cooley
Box 37
Natchitoches, LA 71458
(318) 352-2746
lcooley@natchitochesla.gov

Jane H. Braud
457 East Main St.
New Iberia, LA 71055
(337) 369-2330
jbraude@cityofnewiberia.com

Laurie Toups
632 N. Rampart St.
New Orleans, LA 70112
(504) 256-4848
manager@northrampartmainstreet.com

Glenda Mitchell
1712 O. C. Haley Blvd. Unit 302
New Orleans, LA 70113
(504) 528-1806
ochaleymainstreet@gmail.com

Eva Campos
535 Mandeville St.
New Orleans, LA 70117
(504) 616-7637
manager@stclaudemainstreet.org

Jeff Schwartz
Box 19770
New Orleans, LA 70179
(504) 561-7455
jeff@broadcommunityconnections.org

Lauren Jones
Box 280
New Roads, LA 70760
(225) 638-5360
ljones@cityofnewroads.net

Melanie Lee
828 E. Landry St. #6
Opelousas, LA 70570
(337) 948-5227
tourism@cityofopelousas.com

Kristine Hebert
Box 675
Plaquemine, LA 70765
(225) 687-3116
khebert@plaquemin.org

Charlene Daniels
169 E. Pine St.
Ponchatoula, LA 70454
(985) 386-4923
charlene@branchrealestateonline.com

Kristi Lumpkin
Box 2069
Ruston, LA 71273
(318) 251-8643
klumpkin@ruston.org

Laurie Walsh
Drawer 400
St. Francisville, LA 70775
(225) 635-3873
lauriemainst@bellsouth.net

Danielle Fontenette
Box 379
St. Martinville, LA 70582
(337) 394-2230
stmchc@bellsouth.net

Catherine Olivier
Box 828
Slidell, LA 70459
(985) 646-4322
colivier@cityofslidell.org

Jan Willis-Corrales
400 N. Giles St.
Springhill, LA 71075
(318) 539-5699
jcorrales@cmaaccess.com

Cody Blanchard
409-B W. 3rd
Thibodaux, LA 70301
(985) 413-9886
thibodauxmainstreet@yahoo.com

Kay LaFrance Knight
Box 69
Winnsboro, LA 71295
(318) 435-3781
kaylafrance@bellsouth.net

Anne Butler is the author of numerous books—crime books, children's books, cookbooks, and humor books—and hundreds of magazine and newspaper articles, but her passion is the preservation of Louisiana's unique history and culture. She has a BA in English from Sweet Briar College in Virginia and an MA in English from Humboldt State in California. She lives on one of English Louisiana's early plantations, historic Butler Greenwood Plantation, near St. Francisville, where she writes, gives house tours, operates a bed and breakfast, and is involved in many preservation efforts.

Henry Cancienne resides near Lockport in Lafourche Parish. Cancienne earned Bachelor's and Master's degrees from Nicholls State University in the sciences and education. As a U.S. Air Force Vietnam veteran, retired science teacher, petroleum chemist, volunteer fireman, and police officer, Cancienne has traveled from Denali to Yosemite to Big Bend to Gettysburg national parks and everywhere in between to photograph the treasures of the United States. Recently, he has rediscovered the treasures closer to home in the Louisiana cypress swamps, marshes, rice and sugarcane fields, plantations, culture and unique Louisiana main street communities. Cancienne's photographs have been published in numerous periodicals and books including *Country Roads, Southern Breeze, Country Discoveries, Plantation Homes of Louisiana, Swamp Tours of Louisiana, Louisiana Highway One, River Road Plantation Cookbook, Acadian Plantation Country Cookbook, Hooks, Lies & Alibis, Hot Beignets & Warm Boudoirs,* and *La Meilleure de la Louisiane.* Cancienne states that the theme of his photographic passion is to preserve the present through photographic images before it becomes lost in our ever changing world and society.